The Principles of Modern Web Design

Dr. Ebenezer A. Robinson, Ph.D.

DEDICATION

This book is dedicated to my wonderful children and family who will be delighted to spend any money I might make of it. Thank you for putting up with me. I want to express my gratitude to those who paid money for this book, I am grateful to you and I hope you got your money's worth.

TABLE OF CONTENTS

Dr. Ebenezer A. Robinson, Ph.D.

ACKNOWLEDGMENTS

We the people of the United States, in order to form a more perfect Union, establish justice, insure domestic tranquility, provide for the common defense, promote the general welfare, and secure the blessing of liberty to ourselves and our posterity, do ordain and establish this Constitution for the United States of America.

(Preamble to the U.S. Constitution)

We hold these truths to be self-evident, that all men are created equal, that they are endowed by their Creator with certain inalienable Rights, that among these are Life, Liberty and the pursuit of Happiness.

(From the Declaration of Independence)

Chapter 01

The Importance of Customer-Centered Web Design

As consumers we are continually offered products and services via the Internet. In our jobs, no matter what profession we are in, E-Commerce is being used more and more to conduct business, for training purposes and daily communications. The chapters in this book introduces readers to the basic principles of Web graphics and Web design. The concepts are related to Web graphics, including basic graphic elements and principles of design and creative strategies for developing effective Web-site graphics. These include graphic file formats, preparation of graphics for the Web, and site organization. Reader will develop skills for the integration of graphics into Web pages and gain an understanding of the value of graphics as an Internet marketing element. This book is designed to provide the reader with step-by-step information on how to construct their own Web graphics and Web site. Upon completion of this book the reader should be able to design and develop a simple website and/or become a much better manager of website development and technology.

During the period of the first generation of computer system, the gifted persons and vast teams alike constructed the Web site. These innovative people administered technological system, graphic design and software construction in this new technology. Conversely, the presumption of the people during the first generation of computer system included the satisfaction that the public would derive from the ownership of Web site. This was a period attributed to learning curve.

The practitioners were unable to articulate how their site was performing from the customer point of view. They did not know the connection between the Web site and the profitability of the company. They did not know how to use Web site to conduct lucrative marketing and commerce business. They adopted the defunct concept of marketing strategies.

The second-generation orientation center on the premise that advertisement pertains to excellent marketing tools thus when one sells it online, and they mistakenly assume that customers will come. This led to the several entrepreneur business starts up and they devoted large amounts of capital into costly commercial campaign to steer visitors to their e-commerce sites. Even several reputable companies prefer to put dot com on their document letterhead, they ran costly campaigns to let people recognize how they are so lucrative and in limelight.

Unfortunately, the campaigns approach did not work because the Web design was composite and still misunderstood. For the first time, organizations were building interactive computer interfaces to their products and services. This proved to be a complicated task to perfectly implement. In fact, building a Web site excessively rapid exemplify the probability of being both convincing and uncomplicated to employ. The third generation is about today, the focal point has shifted to erecting powerful Web sites that proffer genuine value, convey optimistic and exert customer experience. Visitors prefer to navigate customer-centered Web sites that promotes rank content, simplicity of use, excellent performance, credibility, and overall approval.

The concept of the customer-centered design articulated that the principle is oriented on presenting optimistic and valuable encounter for all customers. Everyone knows that some customers visit Web sites to locate vital information, while some visit to be part of a community, while other visit to purchase products, or to be entertained. Customer-centered design maximizes the significance of the Web sites via superior design and evaluation that ensue. Customer-centered design is about how several companies are supportive of the need of customers. Thus, organizations concerns about the customer are the followings: (a) customers desires, (b) tools ownership, (c) computer type, (d) brand of software, (e) social context, and (f) organizational context. Accordingly, companies must employ customers understanding in order to structure the Web site designs, as well as verify those designs to confirm that they are meeting the needs of the customers.

According to the concept of customer-centered design, the companies perform preliminary design upfront to ascertain that the Web site has the features that customers prefer. This is done by determining and planning for the vital features while ensuring that they construct those features in a way that customer will comprehend. They conduct customers Web site research. The companies obtain what customers prefer on the Web site from diverse customers, they work together to construct the draft web site, and they correct errors before the companies publish the final Web site. This customer-centered design actually takes less time and money to execute in the end. In short, customer-centered design helps company create the right Web site and construct the Web site correct.

The online practitioners often perform the above concepts to avoid the nemesis that pertains to customer one visit to the Web site and never revisit. For example, the IBM organization discovered that its Web site was not functioning well. The rapid analysis exposed that the search feature was the most infamous function. Further finding exposed that the site was so complex that IBM's customers could not decipher how to locate what they wanted on the Web site. In addition, IBM also discovered that the help feature was the second most renowned function. They concurred that the search feature was useless; many online participants went to the help pages to get support. Consequently, they devoted close awareness to customers' desires; IBM reconfigured the site from the primary stage up to be more reliable in its navigation. A week after publishing the reconfigured site, vast customer dependence on the search and help features plummeted radically and online sales maximized 400 percent. This is just one of several stories stressing the increasing importance of good design.

Everyone must be aware that excellent Web design really affects the bottom line of online companies. The Web sites originated on solid rudiments and wide customers' research can create the distinction between accomplishment and collapse. A lucid, user-friendly, and customer-centered Web site can assist company to acquire excellent appraisals and ratings, and minimize the number of errors made by customers. The customer-centered design minimizes the time one undertakes to get things on the site, and maximizes customer gratification. When the customers prefer site's content and service, they are more prone to tell their family, colleagues, acquaintances, associates and coworkers, thereby increasing the quantity of prospective customers. A grand example of this result is google.com, which has turn into the principal search site. The infamous google.com basically functions better than most other search sites, and customers inform their contemporaries about it. The company conserves their funds by not investing in advertisement.

There is also a robust correlation between increased contentment and increased profits for commercial Web sites. Underscoring this point, NetRaker's research depicts that increasing customer satisfaction by just 5 percent can lead to a 25 percent or greater increase in revenues. This increase arises from customers who can find products and services more easily. These are customers who will return in the future-as well as the corresponding reduction in support costs. The decrease in support costs emanates from a lower number of phone calls, e-mails, and instant messages to help desks, as well as a lower number of returns on products. Web design patterns exhibit a language that you can use in your daily work. In fact, though you may not recognize it, you may already be utilizing some form of pattern language to articulate and communicate your designs. The patterns might replicate your own experience using the Web. You might have selected them up from another site. They could even come from an insight you learned from a successful design you developed and published.

Creative Web design pattern language simplifies how customer engages in shopping and their desires. Companies should response to the design patterns that are implicitly in use and those that does not capture a customer-centered design approach. Several patterns reflect how customers comprehend and dialogue with Web sites. People navigate the Web site with prior presumptions. They take with them all of their previous encounters, proficiency, and perceptive of how several sites works. Customers recognize common indications such as blue links and buttons, and renowned processes such as sign-in and shopping cart checkouts, as dominant ways of making any single site simple to employ.

Amazon.com prefer using graphical action buttons for the featured stores on their website. Some patterns reveal abstract qualities that make great Web sites-qualities such as value, trust, and reliability. Online managers must incorporate value, trust, and reliability into the design of the Web site; they must repeat it and underscore the virtues at every point of contact with the customers. These patterns are known to depict the core of abstract qualities, while the managers and design teams are responsible to integrate those virtues into the Web site. For example, eBay embedded graphical action buttons so that consumers can use the (find it buttons) to locate products from the website.

According to the principle of customer-centered design, the design teams' worldviews are contrary from that of the customers. Thus, design teams must connect their professional activities in unison with that of the customers and embed the outcome on the Web sites.

Chapter 02

Creating A User-Friendly Website

Customers online sometimes desire to quickly navigate from one location to another, but the finding is that search pages often seem complex to accomplish this expectation. In order to cure this glitch, the responsibilities of the design teams included embedding a search action module into every page, employing plain terminology that denotes the search space for typing in words or phrases. In brief, they must install action button that people employ for commencing the search on the Web site. Verification of preceding actions becomes the responsibility of the site managers. If organizations have a large site and want to provide customers the ability to search a subsection, they must add a list of subsections and provide the word that depicts the string to observe. Customers might willingly prefer to employ the search action module when the company made it user-friendly and the search action module materializes on every page. For example, the Barnes & Noble.com implemented a user-friendly search selector that permits consumers to search on precise categories, such as books and music.

According to the infamous discovery, search forms are often ineffective because they need too much precision. The online companies must remedy this glitch by designing a search engine that does not need extreme exactness. In addition, the online companies must take steps to evade *Boolean* searches and precise matches. They must compromise for different stipulations for the same thing. Company must arrange search element to scrutinize transversely all categories by default. Search results should comprise those words that are closely related. The straightforward search forms are excellent when they become part of a conspicuous search action module; hence the online participants enjoy the benefit to observe the attribute on a Web page. Organization must arrange search results that will result in simplicity for

Dr. Ebenezer A. Robinson, Ph.D.

the customers to comprehend what the company offers or locates for them.

According to the concept, online participant often finds search results complex to comprehend, even if these search results are little or several results. This is why online organization must supply their customers with pertinent summaries and arrange search results. They should deliver a clear, concise and arrange search results. In addition, they should implement hyperlinked titled for each hit on the search result page. They must design and employ logs files to adapt the search engine for the most common search terms. Online organization must embed the feature that compromise and correct common misspellings. Companies must endow support for their customers' common search tasks. The tasks of the design teams necessitate arranging search outcomes and update the search database with common synonyms. The site designers must implement the site accessibility pattern to ensure the entire prospective customers, including those suffering from disabilities, can utilize the features of the site. Verification of preceding actions will be the responsibility of the site managers. When writing for search engine, company must provide the Web pages with distinctive HTLM title, as well as simple HTML so that search engines attributes are user-friendly and comprehend by vast customer. Search is indispensable attribute for the entire Web sites. The online managers must erect search features that are valuable and utilizable. The site administrators must devote special attention to the word customer type in, how the organization presents the outcomes, how customers interact with the outcomes, and the organization must ascertain that customers will find what they are searching for on the Web site. The site design teams must embed simple search action module that must materializes on every page so that the customers' searches are more effective and productive.

There is this need to make navigation simple because navigation is an essential component of every Web site.

However, customers soon discover the complexity to locate links and they are not sure whether the links will navigate them to an unwanted hemisphere. When Web sites have distinct community, content, and business sections; it is hard for people to find related topics in each of these sections, thus, the community areas can mature stale. If the online organizations carry the following attributes, such as, content, community, and commerce on the unified browsing hierarchy topics. The online companies must incorporate the three elements into one unified browsing hierarchy, either by directly connecting the three elements, or by integrating the elements into one page. Meanwhile, the site designer should apportion links among the business content, commerce and community Web pages combining them into a unified whole. For example, the yahoo.com site brings content, community and commerce into cohesive. In addition, yahoo site directory contain the availability of united browsing hierarchy. Community is the venue where everyone resides together. Communities elicit another opportunity to strengthen the relationship between the online companies and customers. The online organizations must manage and challenge Web communities to encourage their participants to aim high. In addition, they must challenge Web communities to build stronger community online by convincing prospective customers to purchase. As a community everyone can make a difference.

Customers may call for structured, arrange way of reaching the most important parts of the Web site that is simple to comprehend and employ. In order to alleviate structure anomaly, organization must administer top-level and second-level navigation in a navigation bar along the top and/or left side of each Web page. They must utilize text or both icons and text as links inside the navigation bar. For example, epicurious.com allocate a top running navigator bar, the type that operates across the top of the page on the business Web site. Another example, such as, Microsoft.com site contains a navigation bar that operates across both the top and the left. The links available on the top represent fairly broad topics; the other on the left side wields more precise topics.

Online entities may want to permit customers to navigate through categories of content and present them feedback on where they are. However, to excellently compose tab rows function requires including specific details in the visuals. To correct the preceding, site design teams must be designated to execute tab rows by employing an article tab and indicator line, but with no more than 10 to 15 items, or whatever can fit on one line of tabs. Another solution in this segment authenticates organizations to distinguish an active tab by color and contrasts, as well as through pre-selection. Every organization should produce an indicator line that enlarges across the page to generate the impression that the whole page below the line belongs to the active tab. For example, babycenter.com proffers a well-designed tab rows that elicit visual signals that assist online participants to understand and utilize them more effectively. On amazon.com they elicit indicator line covering the entire width of the page, this epitomizes that the entire content on the page belongs to that tab. In brief, design teams must execute tab rows in order to permit customers to navigate via dissimilar categories of data.

Text hyperlinks are excellent technology for navigating from one page to another, but they are not quite right for representing actions that do something significant, such as authorizing a purchase or submitting a memorandum to a message board. In order to cure text hyperlink glitch, design teams must implement features to signify actions buttons. If design teams utilize images, they should make them materialize as if the online participants can click the feature, they must incorporate a three-dimensional appearance. They should also supply clear and concise labels to elucidate what the buttons will do.

People are widely prevented from finishing a task if the next step is not conspicuous and explanatory. To remedy the preceding problem, on every page that is part of a process, the design teams must embed (a) the high visibility action button, (b) buttons right below the top navigation bar, (c) tab row, and (d) progress bar. In addition, the design teams must replicate the same buttons at the bottom of the content. If vital content cannot be placed above the fold, design teams must create and embed largest action buttons on the screen, and furnish a color that distinct well with the background color. Designer should select button labels that are descriptive and dissimilar from the names of other buttons on the page. They must implement buttons that convey a task forward to the largest ones on the page. For example, the nordstrom.com key checkout button is always conspicuous above and below the fold, this enable customer to always observe how to continue to the checkout. The design teams must execute task critical action buttons to be distinct and show this near the top of the page and underneath the fold, so that customer will be able to discern the process of finalizing their tasks.

Sometimes the customers get lost on Web sites, consumers lose track of the location they are in relation to other pages on the site. The remedy is to implement the Web site locality for breadcrumb links, this usually demonstrate the strategy to employ when navigating from the homepage to the current page and return back to the page. The design teams must employ a string of back links and detach them by a pointing this symbol sign (>) or character. For example, bmrc.berkeley.edu has the bar located at the top of the Web page that exhibits location breadcrumbs, which are responsible to identify the locations. The location breadcrumbs dispense a speedy process to review the formerly seen pages.

Chapter 03

Delivering the best Website experience to Customers

Customers discover value when they navigate the Web sites; consequently they recognize precise products as recommended or featured by the online entities. Otherwise, if the Web site is defunct of advice and suggestions, the product lists can appear insipid and tedious. The online organizations must provide online shoppers with cogent guidance and counsel of what is on the e-commerce site. Thus, innovative organizations must delegate this project to the design teams; hence, they must build category pages that underscore special featured products. Accordingly, the online management acting on behalf of the organization must embed product viewpoint, counsel and product recommendations on the e-commerce site. The management must execute feature products to inform, recommend, direct, and commercialize, such as, show products as top sellers, editor choice, and so on. The online organization should allow visitors to explore by highlighting as many areas of interest as possible. For examples, cdnow.com accentuates various kinds of featured products, cdnow.com represent product guidance. The company shows recent appraisals on featured products and they refer to product as today picks. This company also editorializes about their featured products by depicting them with seductive quality. Amazon.com starts their viewpoint right on their homepage, and they personalize their counsel and advice for visitors. They embed enticing titles in the core of the web page, such as, top sellers, superb quality and get the best. In brief, online organizations must feature products in a variety of ways to inform, direct, recommend and promote sales.

When selecting a product in stores, consumers appreciate hearing about related products that are complementary to or better than the products they desire to purchase. In order to accomplish the same activities in an online requires prudence and planning from consumers. The term cross-sell and up-sell products represent the support, similar product, and empathy the companies discuss to the vast customers. Customers are easily influence and will commit to make a purchase, if the companies are proactive to simplify the process the customers will employ to insert products to a shopping cart without leaving the context of the current page. The design teams must implement visual difference between these promotions and the extra content on the page. A proactive organization will sell the related products again later in the checkout process, in case customers overlooked them the first time. For examples, according to the definition of cross-selling and up-selling, it denotes supporting merchandise that is similar to the current product.

The general hypothesis is that people who prefer wine goblets might also delight in champagne glasses, and nicer goblets. One thing is clear, cross-selling and up-selling links curtail shopping time by assisting them rapidly finalize a transaction. For example, whatever the customer places in the shopping cart, amazon.com supply links, at the bottom, to associated products. After finishing a checkout, amazon.com confers links to products that the customers might have overlooked. Proactive companies often employ cross-selling and up-selling to endorse products related to what customers are already interested in. Personalized recommendations often supply customers with an excellent logic of what is useful versus what is not valuable.

Conversely, personalized advice will not succeed when it entails a situation where customers exert much effort, or if companies are dependent on what customers recognize as insufficient evidence. Meanwhile, online organizations should evade employing inference data to enable product recommendations because the choices of the customers may be contrary. To administer personalized recommendations, the online entities must implement the following: (a) the advice on product must focus on previous purchases by other customers, (b) product commercial must concentrate on past purchases, ratings, and interviews finalized by the customer, (c) embed products accolade on site on product pages, category pages, and personalized advice pages. In addition, (a) give feedback about why company affixes recommendations, (b) embody multiple recommendations, (c) deliver recommendations that customers are familiar with, to help them gauge the quality of the recommendations, (d) embody privacy concerns and how the personalization data will be used. For examples, the amazon.com symbolizes a personalized area that contains all its recommended products.

The amazon.com supports products counsel by concentrating on customer purchases. The netfix.com permit customer to rate movies they are intending to rent, the criteria is that they must not have prior knowledge about this movie. The company includes red stars that identify the average rating by other customers, while stars that are yellow allocate the current customer's ratings. When visitors select their ratings for a movie, the yellow stars exact to what they select. After a customer has appraised a movie, the web site can propose rated movies that may be of interest to this client. Online organizations employ page templates in combination with individual favorites and the product database to extend recommendations to new visitors. Visitors now have the capability to stockpile their individual preferences after they personalize choices or buy something. Organizations are now combining individual choices together with product database to exemplify personalized recommendations. Web site managers must administer the product database through an administrative page in order to simplify the process of appending, eliminating, and editing contents.

The recommendations from other customers are often available, but the method of making sure the community system have liberty from any form abuse is time-consuming and overwhelmed with obstacles. In order to acclimatize to variety of community, the online organizations should supply a two-step procedure to write a review: (a) compel customers to insert review title and text of the review, also affix numerical rating, and (b) let customers observe and correct site recommendation. The design teams must clean out the title and text for profanity and HTML that might navigate to another site. The online organization must hire personnel to evaluate customers-written recommendations and eradicate them if they are offensive or libelous. Once the review is online, furnish a device for other customers to rate the review. Finally, online companies must provide monetary incentive for customers to write the first review, to get consumers to use the community features. For examples, the amazon.com's recommendation community proffers excellent content to the customers.

The origins of the review contents are primarily from other customers and this extends research value to the site, thereby making it a destination for many people, as well as a shopping site. The yahoo video site convey review procedures on the akin page as the input form (a), and it shows reviewers their work, so that they can cross check what they have written before posting it. Amazon.com delivers links to policies and writing guidelines on the same page as the review form. The design teams can: (a) write their review, (b) check their review and (c) submit authentic review. Amazon.com authorizes customers to render remark on varieties of review in a meta-review. The ebay.com depicts numerical ratings, quality and remarks on sellers and buyers. The online organization must apportion a two-step process funnel to assist customers write reviews. They should permit customers to inscribe the review, scrutinize review for conciseness and format the content before submission. The publisher should ascertain that the review conforms to all practitioners standard, rules and because other customers may be affected by the published review.

Customers sometimes desire to purchase several products and convey the items to multiple destinations at once. In order to make this procedure easy, this requires the companies to alter checkout process. The online company must convey products to multiple addresses via action buttons at the top location of the quick address selection page. If the customers click this action buttons, the system will depict new pages that ask for the followings: (a) affix new address action button, (b) embed products in the array, and (c) pick list next to every product. The pick list proffers all the destination options. If there are no existing addresses, as in the case of first-time customers, the attributes instantly convey the prospective customer to a new-address page. For example, the walmart.com represents a quick and simple way to ship items to multiple addresses. The walmart.com requests shoppers if they would prefer to ship to multiple addresses. An address assignment page on amazon.com depicts each product and allocates a pick list of preceding addresses with each. Customers can also access a new address. The order summary pages are widely modified to depict multiple shipping addresses especially at amazon.com. Proactive organizations will provide customers with the option to send products to multiple addresses. They permit customers to choose which products will be shipped where, and they confer a way for them to add new addresses. Before the order is completed, ingenious companies proffer a concise order summary that depicts where entire products will be shipped.

When ordering gifts online, customers desire to write comments to the recipients and they also desire that the price will be confidential and protected from disclosure. If a site does not offer the preceding services, customers will abscond and refuses to procure products or services.

Chapter 04

Making Websites Accessible to Consumers

The immense online sites are exigent for the users including the site managers that maintain the Web sites. The online organization must append a device that will find solution the large amount of site content and how to make the Web site accessible to varieties of people. According to the concept of Web site design, all element and feature are widely intended solely for resolving the problems of bulky content. The principle and techniques that govern the efficacy of pattern group-site genres are the following: (a) employ site genre, (b) evade saving in the file server, (c) database content (d) organize data into browse-able content, (e) involve category pages, (f) adopt content pages, and (g) engage template that describe content. The preceding site design strategy will elicit dynamic publication of the information and maximize productivity. Another solution for content shortcoming is to arrange information into *browse-able content,* with *category pages* and content pages. Each of these pages needs a template to explain its contents.

The page templates characterize areas for navigation, branding, content and related links on every page. Conversely, a site that is not constant from page to page is complex for customers to navigate and hard for site managers to maintain will cause a catastrophe. Accordingly, it is challenging to design Web pages to be consistent because pages are not the same, and many require an update. The design teams must implement grid layout to help define a global template that contain the basic navigation elements, major content region, and any area for related content. They must employ grid layout to line up content modules in the templates. For each kind of page, they must define the individual template that denotes content limits for images and text. Each individual template must use the global template as component of its structure. The online organization should seize the advantages of the reusable structure of page templates because this technology quickly create and publish new Web pages.

An organization would have to integrate the content modules that make it simple to add, change, updates, and exhibit content within a Web page. The content module is a powerful technology that often supports company to publish, manage large volume of content within a page. For example, on *my sun homepage*, participants can choose which content modules they wish to depict. Not all sites will require this height of personalization, though. In *browse-able content* there is availability of solution for discovering content on a site, and in *page template*. The content modules describe how to present page elements in a reliable and user-friendly manner. This pattern explains content modules, a key part of every page template and a way of managing the publishing process. Without the remedy of an excellent system, publishing and managing great volume of content are protracted and error-prone processes. The design teams must define content location in page templates. They must arrange all content into the file system or into a content database. The site managers must administer and monitor content from an administration page. For example, the design teams may employ customer's current position in a site to target content into content modules in a page template. My yahoo epitomizes many types of content modules, including news, stocks, and meteorological forecast. The weather forecast always materializes in content modules on the left, and news emerges in the middle. Short headlines induce customers to click through to peruse more.

The online organization must employ headline and blurbs to compel reader enthusiasm, enabling readers be acquainted with what new events, services, and content the Web site offers. The design teams must create pattern that enable the organization headlines and blurbs writing to draw readers and prospective customers in. In the headline and blurbs structure, content pages require short, descriptive headlines and blurbs to entice or hook customers into clicking for more content deeper on a site. Research demonstrates that systems of hooks are effective if site designers embed the results elsewhere on a site so that visitors will be able to observe them. The web developers posited that the design teams should write a hook in the form of a headline and blurb that enunciates why the content is vital and unique to the visitors. The design teams must stockpile these headlines and blurbs in the content database, along with the longer text, so that this technology can direct the prospect to content modules on dissimilar pages. The organization shall employ the inverse-pyramid writing style to write the site headlines and blurbs. For example, the world news site utilizes database-driven headlines and blurbs to entice readers' attention to the full article on a page deeper in the site. Another example includes gigaweb.com that emphasizes that the excellent location for current research outcome should be in a series of headlines and blurbs. In reality, this whole page is an enticement to steer customer deeper into the site. Accordingly, the landsend.com advertises products on the Web site with headlines and blurbs in content modules, providing a way to underscore new products easily.

In the framework of personalized content, custom-made information can be more functional to people than generic information. However, designing a dynamic site can produce unsatisfactory result if the practitioner refuses to append fundamental structures and designs. The organizations have an excellent assignment of compelling people to personalize the company site before they can utilize it. Successful companies often draw customers in by providing basic but valuable content to new customers that later compels them to eventually personalize. They usually encourage customers to personalize the site from a menu of options, using information that the company collects quickly, such as their backgrounds and area of interest. The organization must gather this information by conducting interviews or by conferring people with the capability to edit their interests. The organization must surmise what other things might interest their customers by tracking the areas of the site that they visit and scoring the information. Online organizations should classify contents and map it to the people who find such contents useful. They have responsibility to structure the site into page templates and content modules that receives content from the targeting engine. One of the first sites to personalize content for each visitor is yahoo.com, for example, my yahoo delivers news, weather, stock quotes, e-mail and many other customizable options. The online company standard is to only target their contents to people, after they categorize it and decide which profile format they will use for each customer. If visitors on site articulate that they are interested in art, for example, the site structure will then direct them to categorize content that is often located in the heading art. Once customers have inserted their profiles, the online company can target content to each person, creating a personalized site. For example, the first-time visitors to my yahoo will observe a simple page that proffers basic content, as well as a note to let them recognize that they can personalize what they observe. Customers are widely invited to create a virtual model at the landsend.com site. The model often provides shoppers with a sophisticated and personalized shopping experience. After customers tabulate a very short form about their backgrounds the msnbc.com provides local news, weather, and personalized stock quotes. A personalized site utilizes page templates and individual customer information to target content modules. The site designers can employ personalization to tailor web sites for individual customer's interests. This is more useful rather than depicting the same information to everyone.

The message board makes the dialogue on a Web site a virtual interaction process, where customers can discuss issues with each other and with the Web site managers. The message boards can engross customers if these technologies

are simple to find and use. Several organization employ message board to create strong customer value. However, manipulating boards to keep them from becoming disorderly requires administrative tools and physical labor. In order to make message board simple to find and use, design teams must build them into the navigation hierarchy and link to the boards from related content. They must furnish the means for visitors to save their favorite boards in their customer profile, and stockpile board links in the browser favorites. The online companies permit visitors seek for keywords in posts, filter posts by date, observe threaded and unthreaded discussions, and sort posts by the name of the individual posting. The online companies provide consumers the capability to read posts prior to signing in or registering. The site managers must ascertain that the consumers know the board rules so that they are not surprised if their messages encounter deletion. The online companies allocate a simple form to post a new message or a reply. The online administrators often have the power to approve or reject posts before posting, especially when a moderated site exist, and they possess ability to eliminate messages on both moderated and un-moderated boards. Meanwhile, the motley fool.com gives customers the capability to save a list of favorite message boards for the next time they sign in. In addition, the motley fool.com extends the ability to search, filter by date, observe each thread, and sort alphabetically. Whereas, the yahoo.com deliver news deliberately permits the rules contain in the message boards to elicit clarity right from the posting page. Accordingly, the motley fool.com embraces a straightforward interface for entering new posts and replies, and this permits customers e-mail replies directly to the original poster, making it much easier for the original poster to respond. In brief, the design teams should create message boards into the navigation hierarchy in order to offer a simple way for people to respond to posts.
There is a sole caveat pertinent to search engines, this include, the intricacy of customers locating a site on a list of search engine results, for instance, if it is too far down the

list. In order to make a site materialize toward the top of any search engine necessitates writing site content in customized ways. In the quest to write for search engine, the design teams often commence by writing distinctive HTML titles for every page. The technology employs the page title in search outcomes.

Chapter 05

Customer Satisfaction and Customer Relationship Management

The Web sites is term as the site genres. The individual genre possesses its own content, needs and audience. This patterns group represents the framework that an organization needs to build several different kinds of sites. Each site pattern elicits concrete ways to differentiate an organization site and describes how to deliver the best experience to the customers. The site genre patterns are sophisticated and fairly abstract. The site genres explain general properties and characteristics of various types of Web sites. Web sites have developed into genres, each with content adapted to their respective audiences. This pattern group reveals how to distribute the best experience to the customers, depending on the genre of the site. The requirements for customers on the sites are dissimilar. The availability of STIMULATING ARTS AND ENTERTAINMENT (A9), Web sites and EDUCATIONAL FORUMS (A8), for instances, vary as much in design as they do in content. Arts and entertainment sites connect people by engrossing them in new worlds and ideas. The educational forums build dialogue around the concerns of the educational community. Organization might draw ideas from one genre to another so that each can benefit from elements of the other. Educational forums may benefit from clearly defined environs that purposely break the rules of navigation to encourage exploration and discovery. Stimulating arts and entertainment sites may comprise educational forums on related topics purposely to advance a depth of understanding. The site genre pattern shapes the core that makes online shopping possible. Several people commence by employing site genres pattern in its most basic form, then enlarge and extend it as needed. They also use it separately or in collaboration with other site genre pattern, such as NEWS MOSAIC (A2), and STIMULATING ARTS

AND ENTERTAINMENT (A9). For example, L. L. Bean provides customers a sense of familiarity because the categories on the site are analogous to what they find in L. L. Bean's physical stores and catalogues. The brilliant colors, clean layout and navigation, and picture in the middle work collectively to draw prospective customers in.

Customers appreciate the expediency of ordering online, but if a site is cumbersome, is vague about its pricing and policies, or does not seem to supply a personal benefit, the customer will leave. The factors that contribute to a successful e-commerce site include conveying valuable content and making it simple to use. The professional that design personal e-commerce should avoid the problems, such as, cumbersome, obscure pricing, vague policies, no convenience and lack of customer benefit. Let personal site make the value obvious to the customers. Depict cogent reason why customers should purchase from the site. For example, Amazon.com supports the preceding concepts of what site needs and even more advanced features. Amazon extends values to customers by obtaining their item preferences and helps incorporate it on the homepage. Let organization design the site with low prices, price comparison, fast delivery, unbiased, ease of use, high quality products review, availability of vast products and hard-to-find products. The preceding statements are the term that denote company up-front value proposition (C2). The up-front value proposition refers to the core value that they incorporate throughout the design and organization of the entire Web site.

Customers are grateful for the convenience of ordering online, but if a site is cumbersome, is obscure about its pricing and policies, or does not seem to provide a personal benefit, the customers will abscond without revisit. E-commerce embraces the promise of making customers' lives easier and more enjoyable. The customers can find products that they otherwise would never come across, and they can order anywhere, anytime, and with only a few button clicks.

People enjoy the satisfaction of discovery, the ease of the process, and the convenience of the delivery. However, on several e-commerce sites, customers do not always comprehend what is being offered and whether it will be of any personal benefit. Organization should make it clear from the start what value the site is providing to the customers and why customer should purchase from the site. Organization should present several ways to find product. Web sites should present customers with MULTIPLE WAYS TO NAVIGATE (B1) because they search for products in many dissimilar ways. Organization should inform the customers about the new and interesting products the site has by advertising FEATURED PRODUCTS (G1) on the HOMEPAGE PORTAL (C1). The organization should assist customers to locate related or more expensive version of products by CROSS-SELLING AND UP SELLING (G2). Another way is to drive more sales by presenting PERSONALIZED RECOMMENDATIONS (G3) particularly adapted to people individual interests and needs. Finally, extend a RECOMMENDATION COMMUNITY (G4) in which customers can respond with feedback and comments on products. By fostering a flourishing community, an organization is partnering with their customers, having them create new content for the Web site, and, in effect, providing everyone with cogent reason for revisiting the Web site again in the future. Customers appreciate the ability to search vast stores of information, observe several CLEAN PRODUCT DETAIL (F2) pages that offer detailed depictions, and compare products. Thus, organization should keep site convenient. The online customers sometimes abandon their order when they discover that the checkout is complicated and not straightforward. In the meantime, the essential goals of the customers are to complete their shopping while the goals of the organizations include closing the sale smoothly and as quickly as possible. For example, Half.com' checkout interface is easy and straightforward. Half.com' permit customers to enjoy logical sequence of steps, shows what stage the customers are in and the steps to aid them to finish.

Meanwhile, organization can evade the dilemma of customer to sign in or creating new account by allowing customers to employ a GUEST ACCOUNT (H3) and then sign in an account after the purchase of product is completed.

Several customers procure products as gift for other people; thus, several organizations provide gift-wrapping, receipts, personalized notes, returns and buying MULTIPLE DESTINATIONS (G5). The online organizations provide ORDER TRACKING AND HISTORY (G7) in case customers want to see their order tracking, examine the status of their product and peruse their previous product. Organization should avoid surprises by permitting customers to be cognizance of their expectation as soon as they start shopping, thus, disclosure about the policies should be placed up front on the site. For instance, organizations should embed the following polices on their sites: (a) returns, (b) additional charges, (c) privacy procedures and (d) security policies. Organization should build trust by instituting a set of FAIR INFORMATION PRACTICES (E3) that people will be compliant with and organization should make these obvious in the PRIVACY POLICY (E4) (Gofman, et al., 2009; Douglas, et al., 2002; Lopuck, 2001). Customers prefer anonymity; they complete their transactions and reveals only important dossier. Furthermore, company should utilize a SECURE CONNECTION (E6) whenever personal or financial information is being transmitted. Additional charges from company may elicit distrust and discouragement from the customers. Hence, on the site, organization should integrate full disclosure of costs at the time of purchase in order to build customers trust. More customers will buy on the site that offers EASY RETURNS (F9) since customer may want to return dysfunctional product to get full refund. For example, the netmarket.com evades surprises by integrating taxes, shipping cost, and handling cost for customers to see even as soon as they add item to their shopping cart. Several organizations distinguish the site so that customers recognize why it is compelling and valuable. The online company embeds the technology of browsing, search tools, and rich elements on the Web site, to provide detail information about the products and services. They make the site accessible to everyone. The home page comprises clear links to the organization privacy, security policy, shipping, handling policy, returns policy and frequently asked questions. Meanwhile, the customers prefer to collect items together and check out quickly, with minimal distraction. E-commerce sites should proffer value, let customers shop and accumulate multiple items, and then promptly check out in a secure manner. CNN's Web site transmits not only the apex news of the day, but also archives of reporting from years gone by. The site varies the content with diverse topics, in short form and in depth. The site persuades readers to use cnn.com as a resource, and it provides a quick lead to what is significant today.

Several readers visit the Web sites to study about their world through news and history. These sites must bring the news their readers want, with the depth and breadth of coverage necessary to connect them, and make the historical record accessible online so that customers can search for older stories. When customers peruse news on the site, they desire to browse for articles that are significant to them, but they also enjoy reading relevant news that they otherwise might miss. Several news sites conceal everything but the most popular news, making it complex to find the more personal topics. For example, CBS Market Watch utilizes embedded links and sidebars to link to stock prices, further search, and stories connected to the current article. Online organization creates a mosaic of news by granting breadth and depth of coverage through a variety of categories and further modification via subcategories. Within each category emphasize the most important article and lead text, while also providing a breadth of articles that might otherwise be missed. Within each article, offer a high-level synopsis first, for people who are looking for a quick read, but also present the more in-depth information in the rest of the article. The organization also link together related news items, whether they are articles, radio stories, or video clips. They archive this information in the same place on the servers for historical reference. Online company should provide a mosaic of news in the article display. The site arrangement should give readers quick access to the vital news on diverse subjects, but it should also allow visitors to drill down for other articles on a subject, as well as archives articles.

The Principles of Modern Web Design

Chapter 06

Customers Driven Web Design

The iterative design process is the process of using current design and readapting it in order to make it equivalent to the desires of the customers. This strategy is widely accepted for designing interfaces. Meanwhile, no design team is perfect. The teams are made of imperfect people who sometimes lack absolute answers. There is always going to be the inadequacy of information about the preferences of customers and clients. The iterative design indemnifies for the inadequacies, by permitting organization to frequently enhance a design. The customers are indispensable with the development of iterative design.

Designers are supposed to keep the customers involve, conduct rapid prototyping and continuously evaluate the designs. The principle and techniques of iterative design comprises the following: (a) keep the customers involved, (b) conduct rapid proto typing, (c) maintenance and (d) evaluation of designs. The act of omitting any of these principles from design processes will cause a major catastrophe. The techniques used in developing iterative designs includes setting measurable goals, frequent refining design prototypes, and testing design prototypes until the final design supersedes the measurable goals. An organization may set the Web site design objectives such as, (a) high-level, (b) strategic, (c) increased customer satisfaction (d) increased sales, and (e) higher profitability. They may also set design objectives to be short-term and tactical, such as, (a) short time for customers to locate items, (b) Web site fewer mouse click to check out, (c) rapid purchase completion, (d) rapid download and (e) Web site revisit. In discussing the concept of Iterative design, it is pertinent to explain that this process embraces a rework of an existing design until it correlates with the needs of the customers. This procedure is widely accepted for creating interfaces, but there is a general consensus that no design team is perfect.

Iterative design is an unending cycle that consists of three steps: (a) design, (b) prototype, and (c) evaluate. Designers should go through iterative cycle many times at the initial stages of design, this should take place before creating final production site and conduct simple prototype evaluation. The main purpose of iterative design processes is to enable the design teams to achieve potential as professional and to effectively design prototype and solve problems when they are inexpensive to amend. In the design step of iteration, design team responsibilities consist reflecting on business goals and customer desires, creating measurable goals and constructing designs plans. The design step is widely based on the teams pondering the business goals, customer needs, creating measurable goals and constructing design concepts. In the prototype step, the design teams build relic as primary scenarios and storyboards, and they create sophisticated running Web sites that exemplify how the site will achieve these goals. The prototype stage correspond to the period when design team construct artifacts that depict a basic scenarios and storyboards of a complex Web sites that depicts the way the site will achieve organizational goals.

In the evaluation step, teams appraise the prototypes to observe if they meet the preferred goals. The outcomes are widely used to update the design in the next iteration, and the entire process replicate until they accomplish the goals. However, sometimes scheduling and budgeting constraints compel work to begin on the final production site before attaining all the goals. They should utilize design patterns to accelerate through each step of iterative design. During the initial design stage, the teams should use the information they learned about their customers, the genre patterns, and other high-level patterns to construct the basic features the site will need. The design team should utilize the more comprehensive, low-level patterns to assist in shaping storyboard and prototype Web pages for precise scenarios. After appraising the prototypes with customers, consumers, clients, colleagues and other team members, the design teams should use the patterns again to find resolutions to the precise problems they encountered. The design team should utilize these solutions in the next design iteration. Prior to working on the final production of Web site, design team should revisit this iterative cycle several times in the initial stages of design and create simple prototypes instead of developed sites. Authentic Web sites can take several weeks or months to complete, and by the time a site is finished and ready for assessment, it might already be too costly and time-consuming to repair. In contrast, the practitioner often develops prototypes in just a few hours or days. The prototypes will not maintain all the features of a finished site, and several features will be faked, but they will be real enough to give customers a flavor of what the final site will be like. In this way you can obtain a lot of feedback about what works and what does nor work. The iterative design is indispensable because the element assist design practitioner to detect problems while they are still less costly and easy to repair. The iterative design guarantees a design practitioner to create a site that contains the features the customer desires. The iterative design permits designer to create those features in a status that the customers can utilize.

As a matter of fact, it is indispensable to fix errors as early as possible. There is empirical documentation in many disciplines that fixing errors in later phases of design can be expensive. In the province of software development, a general principle is that errors cost about ten times more effort and money to repair late in the process than if they are caught in an earlier phase. Several professional in the field of software engineering have even acknowledged costs on the order of 100 to 1,000 times more effort and money to correct problems after deployment. The following are the deplorable reasons of high cost: (a) all the deliverables generated in later phases of design must be consistent with the proposed changes; (b) sometimes one change compels other changes, and (c) most importantly, anything that causes a change in the software source code and HTML is expensive. The iterative design and testing will assist design teams to discover and correct the implementation problems of the shopping cart that make it difficult for customers to check out and confirm purchases. Iterative design assists design teams to locate right features that customer desires and make certain that those features are widely correct and implemented.

A good design process for developing customer-centered sites elucidate that organization should clean out the problems of wrong feature and wrong implementation. The organization should get rid of design that is not useful *and* does not function correctly. The iterative designs are widely created to thrust organization forward in order to attain frequent feedback from customers about site features and their implementation. Design mistakes are expensive, thus, there is great recompense of reward in the future to find mistakes as early as possible during the development cycle. This is why rapid iterative design is so indispensable in the early phases. Iterative helps design teams find and eliminate as many problems as possible before the completion of the site. The organization should engage in site designing mindful of the goals and principle. The goals and principle determine the process of Web site design. Goals are derivative of analyzing the business transactions and customer needs. The design principle recognizes the importance of edge that is derivative from research in human-computer interaction and excellent graphic design.

The organization would have to be concerned with setting measurable design goals. They need to get the site right; this is where business, usability, and customer experience goals come into play. Some possible design goals include the followings: (a) faster task completion (b) successful completion of more tasks, (c) greater ease of learning, and (d) commission of fewer errors. In addition, the rest of the possible design goals includes: (a) abandonment of fewer shopping carts, (b) greater pleasure or satisfaction, (c) more fun, (d) increased visitor-to-customer conversion rate, (e) increase customer repeat visits, and (f) increase revenue.

Studies have shown that in order to increase customer revisits and fulfill business goals, an organization should accomplish usability, and render satisfaction experience to customers. The solution to accomplishing all these goals is for organization to test and measure the methodology. For example, if an organization wants to verify how long does it takes to complete checking out and finalizing online purchase. This is when the task completion time becomes an indispensable metric; thus, an organization could recruit representative customers to tryout the Web site in order to measure the time to complete online purchase checking out. They should use clock to time how long it takes representative customers to finish each task. Also verify if they complete their tasks successfully. Validate if they have problems, and find out commonality among the problems. Determine if the problems occurs in the same places. An organization wants to determine if there are navigation errors, glitch with search features and cross check if current design pattern from other resources can be of assistance. Implement the necessary changes and retest to see if you solved the problems. The responsibility of the design team includes implementing necessary changes and retest to determine if the problems are widely resolved.

Whenever an organization discovers from the server logs those customers who start to post messages in the community section of the site have a low rate of completing the postings. Academic community thought everyone knew that customers are sometimes distracted in the middle of the posting process and tend to follow some tangential links without revisit. This discovery might signify a good place to apply a PROCESS FUNNEL (HI), which will assist the customers go through the steps of completing their first task of posting a message.

Chapter 07

Customer-Experience and Satisfaction Web Design

The opportunities are vast but the tasks are complex on the Web sites, the complexity of the task thus warrants the design teams to understand customers and how customer-centered design operates. Meanwhile, the concept of a customer-centered design exhibit attributes, such as, user friendly, excellent content, performance, trustworthiness and overall satisfaction to the customers. The evolution of Web design consists of the first, second and third generations, and as such, the first generation was a period when mass of Web sites were constructed which resulted in lack of profitability and devoid of customer performance evaluation. In the same vein, the second generation was a period when organization invested primarily on advertisement in order to drive customers to the Web site. Thus, the second-generation strategy was a failure because the Web design was complex, misunderstood and lacked customer satisfaction. In brief, in the third generation, the organizations applied the concept of customer centered Web design, fortunately, organization earn profitability because the site designer focuses on customer desires, experience and satisfaction, thereby depicting excellent content on site. The concept of customer-centered design consist of three segments, namely, (a) principle, (b) processes, and (c) patterns.

The principle is widely referred to as a high level concept that guides the entire design process and help Web designer stay focused. For example, this process required the organization to obtain customers buying knowledge, tasks of the customers, their needs and embed it on Web site. The customer-centered design is a paragon of continuous improvement. The process entails a guide that describes the major steps and milestone to undergo when developing a Web site. One is actually translating the principle into practice. The patterns help organization to resolve repeating design problems, so that designer can employ the solution of the pattern to create sites without reinventing the wheel. Meanwhile, Web design patterns are widely defined as common language or vocabulary that permits organizations and their design teams to articulate an infinite variety of Web designs. The Web design pattern helps organization to resolve new problem instead of wasting time to find solution to previously solved problems. The customer-centered design contains added information set on how-to tips, how to conduct a focus group, how to conduct a survey and how to perform a usability assessment.

The key subjects driving customer center Web design is content, ease of use, performance, satisfaction and brand value. The challenges to be customer centered exist for all organizations. General Motors, for example, must manage its customer experience for more than 300 end- customer supplier, and distributor Web sites. The customer center Web design promotes less time and funds for the future. The beneficiary of the customer-centered design includes non-profit organization, educational institutions and corporate intranet. Organizations should employ a simple, clean, improvement, well design sites and the tool of continuous assessment to create and maintain Web sites. Furthermore, a well design Web sites would improve overall satisfaction and eliminate the following side effects: (a) wasted time for customers, (b) maintenance cost for clients and (c) customers turnover.

Customer-centered design will deliver result, such as, ease of product purchase, allow entertainment, permit membership with site community, maximizes site value, enhances customer experience, and Web owner can elicits compassion. Perhaps one can safely infer, as rightly done by the expects that there is overwhelming empirical support for customer-centered design because it permit Web sites to depict powerful first impression, user-friendly, relevant content and easy to obtain product from the site. The Web site designers prefer the customer-centered design for the following exemplary reasons: (a) it builds on user-centered design (b) cultivates concerns that supersede ease of use and satisfaction (c) helps to combine marketing and usability issues (d) allow converting site visitors to customer (e) foster customer revisit. Similarly, customer-centered design is prominent because (a) it promotes business goals, (b) encourages marketing goal, (c) support usability goals, and (d) endorses customer experience goals. Meanwhile, the dialogue about the nine myths of customer-centered designs should be considered; these are organizational concept or thought processes that opposes customer-centered design orientation.

The principles, processes and patterns defines the procedures to resolve the problems of creating a site that will enable customers to appreciate the content, ease of use, performance, trustworthiness, and overall satisfaction. The credence of customer-centered Web design endures because it increases the revenues of the organization; this foregoing procedure stand on cogent fundamentals thus organizations that conduct extensive customer research are always successful in all realms. A customer-centered Web site is responsible for providing a better reviews and ratings, minimizes errors perpetrated by customers, minimizes the time to find items on site, and enhances overall customer satisfaction. The significance of Web site's content, user-friendly and quality of service this time around is the enthusiasm it inculcates in customers to spread the news to their relatives, colleagues, coworkers and friends, thereby augmenting the prospective customers.

Risk and control are part of business enterprise; they are at the very heart of every business, they help to provide organization with the necessary tools and skills needed to achieve organizational goals. Meanwhile, I am excited to report that customer-centered Web design has been widely implemented by several organizations. The customer-centered system has been widely tested and there were no problems found to date. The concept of customer-centered Web design propounds that organizations should concentrate on customer satisfaction throughout the creation of the Web site. Thus, design teams should find the needs of the target customers, create Web sites for those preferences, and appraise the designs to ensure that those needs are satisfied. They are also responsible to examine the Web site repeatedly with representative customers to ensure that they resolve the mass problems before they escalate to serious problems and before they become expensive to mend.

The management responsibility is to ascertain that the design teams are embedding the correct features on the Web sites and that they are embedding those features right. In recent years, the organization where I work included the definition of customer-centered design into the online bill payment; thus, this escalates customer relationship, satisfaction and enjoyment. Employees are encouraged to be proactive participants to promote the overall customer-centered awareness to management and prospective customers. According to several scholars, organizations may use seminar, training, conferences and continue education to educate design teams on the concept of customer-centered Web design.

The concept about Web site design patterns is a customer-oriented design approach that concentrates on customer gratification, enjoyment, requirements and customer revisit to the site. The primary text expressed insights concerning the design anomalies, how to procure the significance of the problems and execute solution in a concise form. In addition, the text included an explanation that the vast Web design pattern language embraces customers and their preferences. Moreover, one finds that patterns are widely embedded in order to correlate with how consumers understand and communicate with Web sites. Furthermore, the study demonstrated about the patterns that are infamous to the consumers, for example, the three-dimensional buttons and action buttons. These patterns are widely embedded on the Web site for easy recognition. The design patterns present verifiable resolutions to common Web site design problems. Patterns are appropriate to a variety site genre. These patterns are indispensable solutions for navigation, content management, e-commerce, and site performance and entire Web site design. The pattern technology enhances the usefulness and quality of the Web site. These patterns minimize the time for developing Web site. The pattern helps to reduce site maintenance costs. The concept of Web design patterns will help variety of organization to focus on the needs and expectations of the customers.

The concept of Web design patterns give organizations the tools they need to create a satisfying and effective Web site. Patterns explain the site problems in details and the reason for resolution and application of solution. Patterns are widely proven solution to the Web site design problems. Web design team uses language that concentrates on customer, their need, preferences, desire and uses them to create graphic file formats, prepare graphics for the Web, and site organization. In addition, patterns refer to how customers understand and interact with the Web sites. These patterns also contain traits of value, trust, brand and reliability that are included in the design of the Web site. Whenever any customer visit the site these traits are emphasize and reinforced to encourage them. Pattern explains the values of the abstract characteristics and how to embed those traits into the entire Web site. The benefits of utilizing patterns on the sites are that they exemplify experience that the human being as a community have developed and learned.

The Principles of Modern Web Design

Chapter 08

The site designers must know the diverse elements, capable to balance the forces, recognizes customers as people and implement dissimilarity of customers. The customer-centered design process encourages site practitioners to become aware of the target customers group, as well as incorporate their participation in the design process. The design teams and customers differ in the following areas: (a) experiences, (b) thought processes, (c) ideas, (d) skill set, and (e) discharge of individual activities. The online organization must be accountable for balancing the preceding dissimilarities by involving the overall participation of the customers in their Web site construction projects. Accordingly, the design teams must integrate the following elements in the draft and final Web design: (a) target customer knowledge, (b) customer tasks, (c) software available to customers, (d) customers' needs, (e) customer social context, (f) customers preferences, and (g) organizational context. Additional reasons for customer satisfaction were customers-centered design and understanding people, their tasks, the technology available, and how these issues sit within the social and organizational context of the customer and potentially, the client who is having the Web site built.

The online organization must maintain the principles of keeping customers involved in (a) iterative design, (b) perform rapid proto typing, and (c) designs evaluation. Excluding any of the three preceding principles from company Web design processes are often construe as business jeopardy and consequent failure. The followings are the major advantages of employing the principles of iterative design process: (a) elicit cost efficiency, (b) easy to repair glitch, (c) educe timely project, (d) Web site contains features the customers need, and (e) helps to build simple features for customers ease use. Iterative designs exert the concept of measurable goals. Thus, the organizations must continually audit, refine and review design prototypes with consumers until the final design ensue or exceeds organizations goals. The following are the measurable goals that online companies are accountable to accomplish: (a) fulfill customer gratification, (b) maximize sales, (c) minimize time to find items on site, (d) fewer mouse clicks to check out, (e) complete a purchase, (f) customer retention, and (g) customer revisit (Leedy, & Ormrod, 2005; Douglas, et al., 2002; Lopuck, 2001). The iterative design process permit design teams to rework the current site design until it match up to the needs of the customers. In addition, designers employ this process for designing interfaces. The companies employ the concept of iterative design to constantly improve site design. The focus of iterative design is to speedily generate excellent design prototypes that elicit feedback to the online companies. Iterative design helps design teams discover the features customers need, the right features, and ascertain those features are implemented correctly, the right implementation.

The goal is to conduct a credible repetition that may be employed to solve several problems. The iterative design process has three steps: design, prototype, and evaluation. The wise advice is to fix the problems as early as possible. In addition, everyone wants to remedy problems when they are inexpensive to fix. Meanwhile, prior to working on the final publication of the Web site, practitioner must go through the iterative cycle several times in the early stages of design and make simple prototypes evaluation. In the design step, design teams usually consider business goals; customer needs, they create measurable goals and develop design concepts. In the prototype step, design teams develop (a) basic artifacts, (b) scenarios, (c) storyboards, and (d) illustrate how the site will accomplish these goals. In the evaluate step, design teams appraise the prototypes to determine if they meet the desired goals. The outcomes are utilizes to update the design in the next iteration, while the entire process repeats until they achieve the goals. The design teams employ design patterns to help them navigate quickly through each step of iterative design. During the initial design stage, ingenious design teams employ the information they learned about the customers, the genre patterns, and other high-level patterns to execute the basic features the site will need. They utilize low-level patterns to facilitate the storyboard and prototype Web pages for specific scenarios. After evaluating the prototypes with prospective customers, current patrons, and other team members, design teams must employ the patterns yet again to remedy and mitigate problems they encountered. The design teams often apply these solutions in the subsequent design iteration. The storyboards depict the steps a customer would take to complete a task. This storyboard shows how a customer interacts with a site that lets groups of friends find, recommend, and share things with each other.

The online companies that focus on customer centered design embraces agenda that eventually manifest sites that are more helpful, functional, dependable, and gratifying to customers. The customers centered design sites goal is to confer a universal process that online companies can employ when constructing, revising, renovating and updating Web sites. The customers centered design principles assist online companies to concentrate their time and energy on organizational goals. A well-defined process is also useful for the people supplying the funding. It lets the fund provider to recognize what they can anticipate from online companies and what online companies need from the fund providers to construct a Web site that meets their expectations and the preferences of their customers. The customer centered sites design processes are widely customized to the team, the project and overall organization. Several online business owners required their web sites to make their value propositions clear from their tag lines. The business owners believed that the goal of the value proposition is to provide a single, powerful impression of what the Web site is all about.

Generally speaking, development of a Web site can be broken down into seven steps: (a) Discovery phase permit the online companies to know the target customers and their preferences, and assimilating the business and customer goals for the Web site design. (b) Exploration phase is the period for producing several draft initial Web site designs, perhaps one or more will be chosen for further development. (c) Refinement phase calls for enhancement of the navigation, layout, and flow of the elected design. (d) Production phase is the period when design teams develop a fully interactive prototype and a design specification. (e) Implementation phase is the time when team start mounting the code, content, and images for the Web site. (f) Launch is the phase is the period when the entities install the Web site for actual use. (g) Maintenance phase is the stage when the companies start sustaining the existing site, auditing, gathering, scrutinizing metrics of success, and embark on preliminary plan for the next redesign.

The first four steps includes discovery through production, this concentrate on the overall design of a Web site, clarifying what customers can perform on the site and how they accomplish it. One might typify these four phases as the design process. Each is exemplify by speedy iteration with progressive refinement, moving the design from high-level and general to increasingly specific and detailed. During these stages people have found that the more time practitioner spend up front in the tight iterations, the higher the probability that the Web site will meet customer expectations. Meanwhile, in the Discovery phase design teams might maximize the iteration from five to ten times or more on paper. As design teams progress into the electronic depiction often used in the Refinement stage, it might minimize the iteration, perhaps only three or four times. The specific number of iterations depends on how well the design performs and ranks when evaluated.

Online entities are supposed to distinguish their site genres and patterns so that customers may recognize why these technological elements are compelling and valuable. The online entities are infamous for enticing shoppers with the following features: (a) browser, (b) search tools, (c) rich services, (d) rich products, and (e) safeguarding security. They embed genres patterns on their sites that are accessible and facilitate the purchasing process of customers. On every page the online entities deliver obvious links to their frequently asked questions, in the same hemisphere they embed privacy, security, shipping, handling, and return policies. The design teams embed the genres patterns that enable customers to amass products together and check out quickly with zero distraction.

The design teams must generate an up-front value proposition on the homepage portal and deliver clear links for everybody for the site accessibility. They allocate to customers numerous ways to navigate, they append browse - able content, and offer clean product details so that people can compare and contrast diverse offers. They enable customers to select the products or services they prefer by inserting them in the shopping cart, they permit easy navigate via the site quick-flow checkout, and if crucial, customers can seize the advantage of easy returns. The design teams are responsible to affix a frequently asked questions' page, this genres patterns respond to common questions concerning security, privacy, shipping, and returns. The online companies build trust by making their privacy policy constantly conspicuous and available and employing fair information practices throughout the company site genres. Several organizations consistently append daily feature products to keep customers revisiting Web site in order for them to glimpse what the reviewers recommend, and to show them brand new items. For example, Half.com' checkout interface is simple and direct: it lets customers acquire items by taking them through a logical sequence of steps. The system always shows customers what stage of the process they are in, and what the customers have to do to finish the task. Customers prefer to save time, and sometimes they purchase more than one thing. Online managers reported helping customers to save time, and perhaps show them something they might want but have not seen, by cross-selling and up-selling. Shoppers prefer to hear recommendations from others they trust, but they do not want to pigeonhole as a particular kind of person. By using personalized recommendation, you can proffer ideas on the basis of what you recognize someone might be looking for, without resorting to a formulaic recommendation. Customers like assisting others, too. By offering a recommendation community, you permit customers on your site to make their own recommendations. Sometimes customers who want to give gifts may send their gifts to people in many places. By using multiple destinations, they can purchase and send all the gifts in one order. Sometimes customers need to review their orders to ascertain the products they ordered arrived. And if a product that has shipped does not arrive when it should, the order tracking and history features aids customers resolve shipping problems.

Customers are prone to navigate Web sites in several ways. The other issue is about the key navigation tools, sometimes the tools are invincible to uncover or missing, the frequent outcome becomes the situation where online participants will find the site monotonous to use. The online companies must ensure that their visitors complete their goals, to accomplish the preceding they must append the search and browse navigation tools at the pinnacle and start of the page. This becomes equally vital for organizations to embed the next-step navigation tools toward the top, but opposite the start, as well as at the bottom. Ingenious organizations constantly incorporate navigation tools that recount and promote products, so that customers can quickly locate things they might otherwise miss, they usually embed these tools farther down the page. For example, Wal-Mart's site provides consumers with user-friendly navigation and clear signals for locating their way back. They can click on the

Wal-Mart logo to revert to the home-page, on the tab row at the top or the navigation bar on the left to go to another section, or on the location bread crumbs near the top to backtrack. Everyone knows that browsing content on a site can be complex if the data is not organize, or if there are no apparent and consistent navigation indication for finding content and recurring to it later. Innovative companies arrange their content in several ways, in categories that elicit common sense to the customers and in the sensitive ways they think about accomplishing their tasks. The online entities must create navigation tools and signal that permit customers to recognize where they are, where they can go, and how to revert to the initial point. In brief, the online entities must construct each page to exert reading hierarchy so that customers can scrutinize it quickly.

The home-page is valuable to approximately every site as well as site genres. The homepage must satisfy the needs of all prospective and existing customers by establishing the company's identity, while providing multiple ways to navigate. Homepages are the gateway through which most visitors pass during their site navigation. Conversely, the online organization must seduce visitors while concurrently balancing several issues, including branding, navigation, content, and the capability to download quickly. On the homepage portal, designers are accountable to institute and reinforce the value of business site with a strong, obviously stated promise that is fulfilled on every page of the site. The online companies must devote 95 percent of the links above the fold to the visitor groups that consist of 95 percent of the entire visitor population. They must retain the remnant area and links for visitor groups that comprise the remaining 5 percent. The design teams must append extra links in the footer of the homepage to create overt links for each group, plus those in the 5 percent category. An ingenious organization constructs a homepage layout that educes and delineates navigation, content, and downloads quickly. The benchmark is to test organizational homepage design in order to ensure that the design teams have created the right appearance that educes customers' experience. The online companies are accountable to publish homepage that influences visitors, current and prospective customers with content that engross and elicit customer revisit. On various Web sites that people navigate, they are often ignorant of what the company or site offers. The site design teams must embed the value proposition; site advertisement, while both must persuasively articulate the company's exclusivity to customers. The strategies that several entities employ includes inviting team brainstorming, they come together to grow ideas, value proposition and advance the best thought processes into a list of top ten candidates. To incorporate the excellent value proposition, companies must inquire their customers to rate each promise on significance and exclusivity. Consequently, design teams must embed the final value proposition next to business homepage's logo for swift scanning and utmost publicity.

Site genres are reliant on database content, which allows the publication of the data element to the site without the complexity of conveying the files to the server. The consequence is a streamlined publishing process and improved productivity. Even though a site is not database oriented, customers tend to anticipate images and text to be in the same place when they are moving around a site or revisiting to a particular page. Design teams are accountable for arranging the companies' data into browse-able content, with category page and content pages. Each of these pages necessitates a template to explain its content. The homepage of the online company implicitly establishes a blueprint for layout and design of the entire Web site. Subsequently, customers anticipate that they would locate key components of the page in the same places on other pages. The design teams must build a system that obtains the advantages of the homepage portal design. They implement the preceding by creating a family of page templates that communicate to one another but maintain their own differences. For example, Amazon.com uses a global page template to preserve consistency across the entire Web site and the organization also maintain individual page templates to preserve consistency for categories of pages. The global page template is first designed to have the site branding, tab row, search action module, and sidebars appear in the same locations. Individual page templates are then created from the global page template.

Chapter 09

Content modules call for becoming part of the essential graphic design of the Web page. One thing is vital; the length of a content module can commence from a few lines to numerous pages because content modules can be recovered with vitality from files or from a database. Design teams need to recognize the way HTML works, if one content module has excessively much data, it will become exceedingly long and lead to an unbalanced visual design. Design teams must set standards for the length of the content including the length of every page. For text-based articles online companies can employ numerous pages, which let one to break up a lengthy piece of writing into more legible chunks. Assuming advertising supports the site; readable chunks of text broken into pieces across several pages will also exert more commercial impressions. Also offer a method for customers to view all of the pages at once in a printable page because this simply the system for them to print if they want.

In order for a company to build trusted brand on their Web site they must focus on the following (a) content quality, (b) ease of use, (c) fast performance, (d) elicit satisfaction and, (e) brand value. The Web site must carry diverse products or services that customers prefer. The site must be user-friendly and resourceful to produce and carry whatever the consumers want to purchase. The general experience and encounter that customers obtain from a Web site must be pleasing. The Web site must be prompt in its performance. Customers will like Web site to provide commodities and services that are indispensable and exclusive. For example, email subscriptions can be utilized to drive newsletters, focused advertisements, and alerts to interested and self-selected customers. Amazon.com has a feature on its search results page that inform shoppers when new products matching their search criteria materializes.

To elicit trust, credibility and customer loyalty, the organizations embed apparent and understandable privacy policy on their site. They customarily insert privacy policy link in the footer of each Web page. The online company link often retains privacy policy; design teams are known to make it noticeable on the key Web pages, which includes homepage portal, quick flow checkout, and sign-in/new account Web pages. Online companies build trust and credibility when they allow privacy policy to exert a description of what data they accumulate about consumers, how it is used, and how they disseminate with others. To build trust, credibility and customer allegiance requires the company to allow customers to elect how their personal data is employed. If personal dossier is to be used for purposes outside the primary intent, companies should allow customers to decide how it will be used. For example sites need mailing addresses to convey products. Web sites should supply an account management facility to let people appraise and in some cases modify the data the Web site has accumulated about them. The information a Web site has about a person may be imprecise or simply out of date, making an account management system a practical necessity. Web sites should take realistic steps to safeguard all of the information about their customers. Such steps include using secure connections, testing any custom software for potential security flaws, keeping up to date with security-related software updates, having clear policies on how customer information is to be protected internally, and periodically auditing the entire process to confirm that procedures are being followed properly.

One way of administering openness and transparency is by embedding a privacy policy on all Web pages. At a minimum, online companies exhibit privacy policies on key Web pages, such as the homepage portal, major access points, the quick-flow checkout page, and any Web page where large personal data is collected, such as sign-in/new account. Online companies build trust, allegiance and credibility when they give consumers the choice of how they employ e-mail addresses of customers, particularly for e-mail subscriptions. An option is to let customers utilize one-time guest accounts. Online companies build trust and credibility when they employ secure connections for any transaction relating to sensitive data, including passwords, personal finances, and e-commerce purchases. Web sites should also elicit an account management facility; letting people observe what information the Web site currently conserve about them. For instance, the Exploratorium is a hands-on children's science and art museum in San-Francisco. Its Web site has a small and simple privacy policy, explaining the kind of information that is collected, how that information is used, the exception conditions, and the fact that personally identifiable information from children is not requested.

A further way of building trust is to exhibit information about the online company, such as, their employees behind the Web site including crucial real-world information, such as a mailing address, 24 hours phone number, cell phone numbers and fax number, as well as background profiles on the company and the people in the company. When customers encounter your web site for the first time, they have three questions in mind: Who are you? What do you do? Why should I trust you? The (About Us pages) are one way the Web site can help answer these questions. About us pages accumulate background information about a Web site, presenting information concerning the people, the organization, and/or the company behind the HTML. About (us) pages are also imperative for instituting trust because they allow customers to recognize the availability of real people and a real company behind what most people call virtual world. The online companies must employ *about us* pages to elicit information personalized to customer demographics, interest, and needs. For example, the Lego

About Us Web pages incorporates a page about fair play, explaining why Lego has to protect its trademarks, brand, and what fans may and may not do when creating their own Web sites about the toy. Contemporary companies embed secure connection in order to help protect sensitive personal data, and safeguard financial data that the customers send to the company's coffer. Secure connections should be widely used in all Web pages where the customer enters sensitive or financial data exhibited for the customer. They must embed secure connection in places such as sign-in/new account, quick flow checkout, important process funnels, account management and any web page dealing with financial data. Resourceful companies implement obvious labeled action buttons to permit customers to know that their transaction is secure. For example, at Half.com, the checkout procedure is conducted over a secure network and connection. Half.com underlines this fact by placing a secure shopping icon at the top right of the checkout pages.

The e-commerce is the technology that permits people to have the ability to find and purchase product online. The commercial aspect of the Web is the cogent reason for consumers to navigate online. In order that customers might engage effectively on the Web, the site design must generate clean, uncomplicated interfaces and support for common assignments. For example, Amazon.com deliver answers to deal breakers on key pages so that customers will cursorily receive answer to their questions. The e-commerce site contains uncomplicated shopping experience for customers with subsequent personal benefits. Once shoppers have accumulated all the products they desire to purchase in a shopping cart, e-commerce site shows how to have them check out, employing a quick and easy process funnel. The e-commerce organization primarily confers protected link to the customer before offering them a guest account or inviting the customer to register on a sign-in/new account page. The e-commerce company dispels concerns about the proprietary data that the customers are inserting, they also provide answer to questions that consumers may have about particular policies. The e-commerce organization supplies broad view of the process and provide their privacy policy context, sensitive help, and they respond to customer questions by embedding answers to frequently asked questions. The e-commerce company customarily provides links to return policy to simply customer easy returns. On e-commerce site, there is availability of high visibility action buttons because online companies carry massive data more than adequate to contain on a single screen. Everyone knows that e-commerce site contain a progress bar on each page this enable online shoppers to recognize their exact vicinity on site. The e-commerce company is infamous for permitting customers to utilize quick address selection or multiple destinations that encourages a venue for gift giving. E-commerce site often contains a segment where customers elect a quick shipping method; this quick shipping method design is excellent on the same page. Meanwhile, on the subsequent page, is where customers will find an order summary, including links for the people to employ when performing corrections, thereafter, the company may ask the customers for their favorite payment methods. Finally, e-commerce organization permits customer to validate their orders with an order confirmation and thank-you page. The e-commerce site permits company to reduce their customer support calls; the supporting strategy includes steering online users to order tracking and history.

Everyone knows about the availability of personal e-commerce, self-service e-commerce and government e-commerce. Conversely, whatever the name tag personal e-commerce bears they concentrate on efficient web appointment, whereas intranets embraces what would assist online users to finish their assignments. One thing is important, online participant enjoy finishing the assignment they commences. The following are the dilemma that online participants discharging their assignments may encounter: (a) misleading links, (b) extra steps may prevent achieving task, (c) extra content may prevent goal accomplishment, and (d) challenging diversion. The online organizations must eradicate the amount of glitch level preventing the accomplishment online assignment. They must supply a progress bar that will inform customers concerning their progress in the process funnel. Everyone knows that online companies must eliminate irrelevant links content and buttress the brand. The site design teams must incorporate pop-up windows to exert information, without misdirecting visitors away from the process funnel. The site design teams should embed efficient back button that momentarily save data on each page for subsequent depiction whenever the customers press the back button. Web site developers can minimize the number of steps needed to complete a task, by keeping them between two and eight. Remove unnecessary and potentially confusing links and content from each page, while underpinning the brand to maintain a sense of place. Use pop-up windows to offer extra information, without leading people out of the process funnel. Make sure the back button always works so that consumers can correct errors. Make it clear how to proceed to the next step with high-visibility action buttons. Prevent errors where feasible, and present error messages whenever errors do occur.

The grid page layout is infamous as the page template pattern. Meanwhile, the components of page layout include navigation bars, search action modules and content modules. The online practitioner often create grid layout and embed the elements on top of the fold, this permit consumers to glance the element without scrolling up or down. The design teams must embed the layout to highlights the front element that participants primarily encounter when they navigate the Web page or a clear first read. They must insert several item, recover content, and modules in the grid. The site managers must have definite oversight over the layout of a Web page they are accountable for preventing the modules that contain erratic length. Several designers employ HTML tables to execute grid layouts although they can be slow to upload if designers utilize older Web browsers. The designers might employ the strategies of breaking large tables into little separate tables this is done in order to increase the load speed.

The design teams are infamous for assigning the site search tool in a stationary hemisphere while locating it in every Web page above the fold on the top left, middle or sometimes on the right segment. In writing the content for search engines, the design teams must create online search attributes, customers business site content, eventually embed search action module into every Web page. The organization must label the button that commences the action such as search or go and call it action button. The online organization must embed straightforward search forms on the business site this permit consumer to logically fill out form. The design teams must embed organized search results page because this is the recipient of the usual results. The search action modules formulate the features simple enough for consumers to locate the search feature on the site. The company must create an easier search system that accommodates customers' amateurism. They must elucidate how customers can evade customary errors with the search entry forms. The uncomplicated search forms become the part of a visible search action module that visitors can effortlessly find items on a Web page. The organized search results permit customers to find ease in comprehending what the search has deduced for them. For example, Barnes & Noble.com provides a search selector that allow customers to search on specific categories, such as books and music.

The design teams must create a visible search action module and straightforward search form this will help resolve search engines dilemma that confront site visitors. In addition, they must curtail the search results so that the results become pleasant for customers to understand. They must structure and arrange search results because this will exert logical reasoning. This pattern covers ways of organizing and categorizing search results to make them more valuable to your customers. This is applicable to both local searches on your site and Web-wide search engines. The organization may encourage the practitioners to design for multiple ways of navigating browse-able content. However, what about cases in which a site offers content, commerce, and community all around the same topic or topics? This pattern must exert a navigable design for sites that have these features. The multiple system and navigation strategies elicit consistent attributes for browsing and searching a Web site. The organizations must create browse-able content and search action modules that would generate the essential for constructing a browse-able formation and uncomplicated search. The design teams must embed navigation bars in order to exert path for customers to enter to the core of the business Web site. The organization must create pattern to permit valuable navigation bars to benefit online customers.

When the navigation bars contain site images, the design teams must obtain certainty that the business site actually exercise quick downloading images. The navigation bars of every company that embrace obvious links are renowned to achieve highest clarity. The online organization must require the design team to construct HTML power that will accept color background, which is quite different from body copy of the background color. In order to circumvent the protocol of obvious links, the design teams must locate the navigation bars to the left side; they must also curb underlines and switch the color of the links to other color instead of blue color. The customers often yearn to visualize the tasks they are working on, thus, the design teams must embed tab row and situate it on the top-level navigation. The design teams must eliminate clear first read from the Web page customary left corner; this would permit the navigation bars to become conspicuous.

Web site developer should improve the performance of the site by controlling the most important pages and focus his/her efforts on tuning those pages for download performance. Developer must curtail the number of files that absolutely must be downloaded for each page. He/she should seize the advantage of features in HTML and in Web browsers that curtail the number of images customers have to download. In addition, transfer slow-loading objects from the most important pages to other pages, and provide links to and previews of them instead. Similarly, online companies must apply HTML power to utilize HTML instead of images. They must employ reusable images throughout the site so that the company is enabled to amortize the download cost. They must employ a low quantity of files in combination with fast downloading images and separate tables to greatly enhance the download time of each Web page.

The vital pages one can optimize for a low number of files are the homepage portal and the quick flow checkout. For example, the yahoo's homepage embraces minimalist orientation that contains few images, enhancing it to fast download. Images are often the slowest-loading component of a Web page. Reducing the size of an image can have significant impact on how customers prefer revert to your Web site. For example, the geocaching.com utilizes micro images that are designed for download. Another way to enhance Web site download speed is when a Web site developer use a combination of methods to speed up the downloading of images. Apply these techniques-changing the image file format, reducing colors, cropping and shrinking, using higher compression, and using progressive-scan or interlaced images-to the image itself. Other strategies apply to how the image is utilized on a Web page and help improve the perceived speed of loading the image, such as integrating the height and width attributes in the HTML, using the ALT attribute for the IMG tag, and combining small images that are near each other into larger images. A different way to enhance Web site download speed includes employing the pattern of separate tables, the strategy of simplifying tables and separating them into small tables enable them to display faster on Web browsers.

Dr. Ebenezer A. Robinson, Ph.D.

Chapter 10

The design teams must utilize this pattern of separate tables alone to maximize fast down loading of Web pages. Otherwise, the design teams must employ this pattern of separate tables in collaboration with low number of files; fast-downloading images, reusable images and HTML power patterns to elicit fast downloading of Web pages. For example, the petaonline.com displays separate tables in action; at the top table is what consumers observe while the Web page is down loading. While at the bottom is another table depiction that the customers observe after the page has finalized loading. Several organization employ separate tables to permit items to be loaded first at the top segment of the Web pages. They insert vital navigation elements and content in the first table so that online participants will observe them first, while the remnant of the page is loading. The followings are term as reusable images: (a) logos, (b) navigation bar, (c) stylistic and (d) accent graphics. The primary concept is that if online users revisit a Web page they have navigated before, this will be faster to depict because there is no need to re-download. A Web browser must download brand new image and Web pages in order to store them in a cache. To increase Web site download performance, online site design teams must embed Web pages to utilize reusable images. These images will be contain in a cache attributes of the Web browsers and will be faster to exhibit during the next revisit or navigation by customers. For example, lowestfare.com converts several reusable images for stylistic purposes, this includes the small images that are employ to make curved tabs in the tab row and the small white arrows to mark dissimilar travel services offered.

Sometimes site visitors want to probe deeper into a certain subject that materializes in the text, or they desire clarification but do not want to go searching for it. Meanwhile, the embedded links situated off to the side or links located at the end of the text sometimes need the incorporation of context, this is essential for readers to comprehend how they relate to precise sections of the content. Consequently, the design teams must append links within a text passage to permit an extra free-form discovery. They must employ descriptive, longer link names to let customers know the destination where the links will navigate them on the site. They must also maintain the number of embedded links available in a page of text available on the low segment, so as not to overwhelm readers. Site designer often employ pop-up windows to represent additional information while maintaining the context, and to avert visitors from jumping to other pages. Online entities must implement obvious links in combination with embedded links because this simplifies the way the customers skim through text. The design teams are famous for creating embedded links that contain descriptive longer link names; cogently to help online participants to decipher the destination the links will pilot them on the Web. The pop-up window assists and prevents online users from losing the context of the existing page. Meanwhile, embedded links are infamous for navigating from one web to other web sites. In brief, the design teams must employ external links to insert label and assemble these links to administer site consistency.

Most e-commerce sites have links to other Web sites. These external links deserve to be widely treated in a special way. This will allow customers to comprehend that they are navigating to other Web sites that are dissimilar to the current Web sites. Accordingly, external links can elicit trust and credibility among company customers. This external links also reduces the amount of work required to implement new content. All organizations are required to embark on special care, to inquire permission from external site operators, learn policies contain on page addresses and dynamic content creation so that they can avoid common link rot (Douglas, et al., 2002; Lopuck, 2001; Gofman, et al., 2009). The online organizations shall be responsible for allowing their customers to know that they are about to be conveyed to an external site, this is possible by openly marking each link, or by inserting external links in a well-marked area on the page. Responsibilities of the design teams include embedding pop-up windows for external links to maintain the context of the site, so that the site participants will not lose their places in the online activities. The external links contain the attributes responsible for directing people to other Web sites. They allow people to observe the collaboration of business Web site and their interaction with other individual, locations, items, products and services.

The practitioner often creates text hyperlinks predictable and explicable in terms of the Web pages to which they link. Otherwise, when browsing, customers will repeatedly pursue links; arrive at something contrary that does not interest them, and repeatedly *bounce* back and forth in aggravation. Consistent with the standard, online company must utilize descriptive text hyperlinks with longer link names that operate as a preview of the linked page. Company must also construct the link name by abbreviating the linked page in a few words. They have the obligation to employ familiar language, and be sure to distinguish links that have analogous names. Finally, companies must ascertain that any links with long names that word-wrap is clearly distinguished from other links. For example, the cnet.com is a web news network that integrates the link on the left side of the page and when the links are press upon this feature conspicuously depicts the location the online users will navigate. The site design teams must embed descriptive text hyperlinks with longer link names to assist online participants to link to varieties of other dissimilar content pages.

The site feature is not always obvious about which bits of text are links for customers to utilize or click for site navigation. To correct this glitch, online companies must adhere to the use of blue underlined text for obvious hyperlinks. They must evade employing blue or underlines for anything other than Web links. Online companies are required to construct obvious links more gorgeous by utilizing dissimilar font sizes and styles. Each online company will be responsible to employ the title attribute with text links in order to enhance site accessibility, and they must evade utilizing colors connected with color deficiency. Design teams will be required to employ diverse colors or links if they are designing a Web site as a puzzle, as an art piece, or for fun. For example, the lugnet.com permits online users to speedily know which links the people have previously navigated and those ones waiting for navigation.

The remedy for unfamiliar terms and link names compels the online organizations execute familiar language that their target customers understand. The plan of action is to scrutinize and interview representative customers so that the companies can sympathize with the way they observe and comprehend their worldview. Online companies are normally required to employ strategy such as card sorting, category identification, and category explanation to elicit how they arrange, structure, and explain things. Companies must employ all of this information to construct content and links that their customers will find explicable and predictable. For instance, the edmunds.com is a user-friendly site, where the company employs simple, familiar, and easy language to exhibit, carry and advertise their appliances or automobiles products.

Customers are candidate to engage errors and produce erroneous data when confronted with online forms that have little structure, further include no formatting directions and are not designed to account for errors from the start. To prevent errors, companies must embody hints about what kind of text input they expect from their customers. The responsibilities of online companies here include evolving fields showing formatting, representing sample values in the fields or by proffering explanatory text. Definitely, companies should allocate flexible formatting and have the computer establish the correct format. In addition, company must make it apparent which fields are required and which are optional so that customers will not have to guess. For example, myciti.com safeguard against errors by promoting field that are absolutely substantives. The design teams must execute and insert those patterns that prevent site errors. To accomplish this project, they must insert formatting and distinguishing samples in the field section where this is required besides include the optional field.

When customers perpetrate mistakes, with decorum, company should inform them of the problem and how to gracefully recover, or this error state may persist. Customers are often looking for committed companies that will indicate meaningful error messages in recognizable language without transferring blame and without trivializing the problem with humor. As communication is essential, companies should elucidate the severity of the problem and apportion steps that customers can take to recover. Proactive organizations exhibit the error message in close proximity to the problem area, and emphasize it in order to make it stand out visually. For instance, Dell Web page manipulate errors in the checkout with two error messages, these error messages are positioned near the problem area. These error messages depict the problem and what customers must accomplish to fix it.

Practitioners readily acknowledges that sometimes customers perform or experience the following activities on the Web sites: (a) click on links, (b) inscribe in URL, (c) discovers non-existent bookmarks of pages, (d) not *finding a page, and (e)* receiving error message or *error 404*. To correct the foregoing, the online companies should apportion a custom page not found Web page that makes it simple for customers to browse or investigate for the content and everything they expect to find during the navigation. For example, Microsoft has a distinct page that it displays if the technology cannot find a page. This page aids consumers who may be lost by providing a meaningful error message, a site map with an overview, a search form, and basic navigation to the main portions of the Web site.

The slow sites are aggravating to embark upon by any online participant. A slow homepage can have a major shock on customers' first experience with a site. The customers might abscond without purchasing or comprehending what the companies have to offer. There are still availabilities of customers who are still navigating the Web site with slow and analog modems. Even if one publishes a business site, many of the customers will be navigating the site from home, after work hours, or from a laptop on the road. The vast techniques are available for online companies to incorporate in order to speed up the Web site and elicit excellent performance enhancement. For example, to alleviate the nemesis of slow homepage, the yahoo.com embraces a small list design that contains few and little images, this enable yahoo homepage fast to download. Site designer create their web site pages faster to download because they reduced the amount of files available in those pages.

The catastrophe of slow download will ensue with the Web pages that contain several images, audio files, applets, and plug-ins. To cure the foregoing, online organization must maintain low number of files ameliorate slow download. The design team must designate the vital pages and concentrate their efforts on modifying those pages for download performance. The design teams must diminish the quantity of files that must be downloaded for each page. Innovative organization must seize the advantage of attributes in HTML and in Web browsers that diminish the number of images customers have to download. In addition, design team must convey slow-loading objects from the vital pages to other pages that are meant to be fast; implement the replacement with links and previews technologies.

Everyone is familiar with the concept that the large images elicit time consumption attributes that causes slow download. In order to exert fast downloading of images, entities must implement a combination of strategies to speed up the downloading of images. The following strategies are effective for fast downloading images: (a) revise image file format, (b) alter colors, (c) employ cropping and shrinking, (d) add higher compression, (e) append progressive-scan, and (f) tie images into image. Online organization are encourage to integrate compressing image strategies such as (a) build height feature in the HTML (b) width attributes in the HTML, (c) develop the ALT features for the IMG tag, and (d) merge little images in close proximity into larger images. For example, the geocaching.com site employs micro images that are widely optimized for quick download.

The finding is obvious that the Web pages with lengthy, complex HTML tables take a long time to exhibit in the Web browsers. To correct this dilemma, design teams must tear and isolate vast HTML tables, they must execute and insert smaller separate table so that the download will become more efficient and the display of each table is more independent. For instance, the babycenter.com contain separate pages one in the top segment and the other is located in the bottom segment of their page. This strategy of babycenter.com permits customers to become recipient of feedback while the bottom table progressively loads.

The online practitioners are convinced that images are vital to excellent Web site design because they apportions visual sign about interaction and how the page is arranged. They are aware that Web pages with varieties of images are slow to download. The excellent cure for cumbersome images compels design teams to embed HTML power features instead of images on the site. They must search for the functional and attractive location on the Web site because this is the excellent sector to embed the HTML power. For example, the online managers who designed the Lincoln Highway site utilizes HTML features instead of images to handle lay-out, background colors, and bullets. The result is a simple and clean design that is fast to load.

The online participants are conscious that a Web browser must slowly download every new image when this is the first encounter. The problem of slow downloads are resolved when design teams create the Web pages to utilize a crucial reusable images. These images will cached by Web browsers and will be faster to show the next time they are observed because they will have already been downloaded. For example, MP3.com uses various small, reusable graphics to accent its Web pages, including its logo, small question marks for getting help or assistance, small plus signs for adding music to a personalized Web site, and small chevrons for playing the music. The online managers in organization should be compelled to curtail the amount of files that must absolutely be downloaded for each page, seize the advantage of attributes in Web browsers and HTML that diminish the amount of images consumers have to download. They must convey slow-loading objects from the vital pages to other pages consequently supply links to and previews of them instead. The online managers must employ reusable graphics to accelerate the download process of the web browser; Web pages so that the frustration of the customers will be widely eradicated, this will boost sale increase, gratify customers, elicit patron revisit and bring about customer retention.

Chapter 11

Resourceful companies often dispense to customers obvious signs early in the shopping process that the site has gift-giving alternatives and services, so that they can shop for that reason. On the checkout page, the ingenious companies accommodate a button that pilots customers to a form where they can insert notes and select gift-wrapping options. In addition, on this form, they embed a button that return customers back to the order summary page, where they can appraise their whole order, including gift alternatives. When purchases are finalized, the order confirmation page will list the entire order, including gifts, in case customers desire to obtain information for documentations. For example, marthastewart.com composes the process for customers to discover gifts buying for their loved ones for an array of special occasions. The web site apportions gift-wrapping and a gift message on every order. These attributes, combined with the site's spotless design and navigation and the excellent services of gift-giving site. In this example of the gift-giving process funnel, walmart.com furnishes the simple to append gift-wrapping and personalized notes to each gift. An organization that implements gift idea can assist customers find the right gift. The online entities authorize customers to select which purchases are gifts or personal. In brief, online organization must provide customers the option of wrapping each gift and typing in a personal message.

When customers situate online orders, the aspects about order status and shipping become significant. If this data is not easily available online, the cost of processing customer inquiries increases significantly. Online entities must embody history and order tracking on the Web site.

Meanwhile, online companies often requisition customers to sign in to review their orders and amend them. The online organization bequeaths customers an access to an order history that categorizes orders as pending, shipped, or completed. These businesses must depict the chosen orders chronologically; listing the order number, as well as the contents of the order provided the list is concise. For pending orders, they have the attributes that indicate each item's availability; they allow customers to perform adjustment on shipping, billing, quantity, products and options. For products the companies have already shipped, they must tolerate order tracking by interacting with the shipper's database. They must show the history of the shipment schedules. In this situation, the nordstrom.com web site exhibits clear order detail, together with product shipping destination, product details, quantity, price, gift options, shipping processes, charges, tax, and totals. In another example, the shutterfly.com web site allocates a convenient order history with status and order detail. The amazon.com contains the previous and amendable orders. Whenever the company finally ship customer products, the site commences to administer order tracking. Online companies must safeguard and offer a secure order tracking and history structure in order allow customers assess their past and awaiting orders.

The online managers must execute the concept of recommendation community on the ecommerce Web site. This type of recommendation community prevents customers from casting away their confidence in their choices. The recommendation maximizes sales. The organization must promote the concept of personal ecommerce. They must grant customer shopping gratification, customization, sole need, and personalized content. The online managers must insert personalized content that will enable customers to elicit and express their desires. This organization must interview several customers in order to deduce their needs and convey them via a process funnel. The managers in organization must exerts personalized content that is oriented on consumer profiles to create merchandise category pages and clean product details. The organization must insert community conference tool this will assist to supplement consumers shopping experience. This organization must procure customers voices, skills and opinions then pass on this knowledge as personalized recommendation to other customers.

Customers often need to finalize highly specific tasks on web sites, but pages with tangential links and various questions can become an impediment to carrying out these tasks successfully. Proactive online entities must seize the advantage of site process funnel and extend gratuity tutorial programs to assist their customers because they need such help to finalize a complex task on the business sites. The site design teams must diminish the number of steps requisite to finalize a task, curtailing them between two and eight. They must eliminate redundant and potentially confusing links and content from each page, while highlighting the brand to maintain a sense of place. They must employ pop-up windows to represent extra information, without diverting people out of the process funnel. The site managers must ascertain that the back button always functions so that customers can repair errors. The site design teams must plainly implement attributes to proceed to the next step with high-visibility action buttons. The site managers must preclude errors where possible, and supply error messages to the customers when error materializes. As an illustration, Dell exerts a process funnel comprising of several logical steps that direct customers to rapidly configure and buy a personal computer. Information in a pop-up window exhibits additional details but retains customers in the funnel so that they can prolong to completion. Many web sites exert a progress bar to allow customers know where they are located in the process funnel and how much beyond they have to go. A process funnel authorizes people finalize their goals by breaking down complex tasks into a small number of steps, using pop-up windows for complete data, and minimizing the number of links to only the critical ones, so that people remain focus and alert.

The sign-in/new account procedure has the problem of manipulating both revisiting customers, who sign in and the company comprehends them as individuals procuring personalized content, and new customers are on the site to obtain an account before they commences on the site. According to the concept of sign-in/new account, the organization must gather the minimum amount of data they need to generate new accounts. They must device clear fields that are requisite and which are optional. The online companies must preclude errors where possible. They must furnish authentic privacy of information on organization web sites. Equally important, site design teams should insert a process for handling customer-forgotten passwords. Companies should avoid compelling first-time customers to sign in too early. For example, the google.com exerts an easy sign-in, the criteria such as customers must previously have an account, or if visitors generate a new account on the spot. Meanwhile, if an organization wants visitors to create a new account, they must simplify the procedure by minimizing the number of likely mistakes and adequately maintaining it as soon as possible. The ebay.com frames a security questionnaire in case customer forgets his or her password. Consequently, they employ the security questionnaire to email or reset the password if the customer forgets what it is. In general, the procedure of signing into a Web site should proceed as follows: (a) visitors access an ingress point to sign in, (b) customers recall the password sign in and continue, (c) visitors may compose new account and then proceed, (d) revisiting consumers may insert wrong password are consequently blocked from continuing, and (e) revisiting customers may obtain help recalling the password or to reset the password.

Many customers will be put off and possibly abscond the site if they have to generate an account to utilize the Web site. However, companies need data from customers in order to support them in their tasks. The online businesses provide new visitors the alternative of creating a guest account at the end of a process, rather than compelling them to create one at the beginning. For example, the healthgiant.com permits its customers to acquire products as either by guest account or registered members. When purchasing as a guest, customers are reassured that their personal dossier will be employed for only processing the order and will not be kept in the company's database. The usmint.gov checkout apportions customers option between continue checkout and member checkout. The first option directs customers to the billing address page, which guarantees customers that the information submitted, are employ only for the purpose of fulfilling the order. In addition, the outpost.com authorizes people without accounts to make purchases first and then create an account, if they prefer. They also administer an accelerated checkout process for customers who previously have an account. The taxpayer.com web site elucidates obviously to its customers that there is no membership requirement on the site. The online organizations must actualize account creation to remain optional, and conveniently place it at the end of the process.

Customers need to observe and administer the data a Web site retains about them. Organization must implement a single page that collects the entire customer's account information in one place. They must employ a task oriented organization system to let people observe and adjust their data in the context of specific tasks. Organization must execute account management system because the system employs a secure connection to safeguard each customer's personal data. The account management system steer customers through the steps needed to see and modify their information. In the buy.com Web site, there is availability of account management page that permit consumers to observe and update entire information that the company administer for them. Customers enjoy the benefit to update their e-mail address, payment data, and shipping detail, together with the status of their previous and current orders. The cdnow.com exhibits customers their account data in context, when they need it for a precise task. For example, customers can modify their credit card data at the checkout instead of reverting back to the account information page.

Chapter 12

To supply personalized services, Web sites deserve to
recognize who their customers are; they can achieve this by
tracking their presence on the site. Companies might employ
persistent customer sessions to develop personalized
services. They have the option to utilize temporary customer'
sessions for brief transitory data or when privacy concerns
supersedes, such as on self-service government web sites.
Conversely, companies often implement persistent customer
sessions for permanent data, or when the companies want to
know the identity of the customers. Online companies must
evade placing any sensitive data in sessions. They must
utilize cookies for recognition purposes, this is not
appropriate for authentication. The term persistent customer
sessions refer to a tiny piece of data that they transmit
between the web browser and the web server. This data are
employ by practitioners to create personalized content and
services. In order to safeguard against identity theft and
protect the consumer dossier, online organizations must
embed secure connections, firewall software, authentic
privacy policy, and fair information practices.

Companies might desire to demonstrate to the customer
extra information, while maintaining context and keeping
the customer's web browser intact on the same page. The
online companies must implement routine pop-up windows
for portraying unconnected information when consumers
ingress or exit the web site. They often utilize link-oriented
pop-up windows to exhibit connected data in a new window,
while maintaining context. Online companies should reduce
the use of pop-up windows. For example, the
guir.berkely.edu studies elucidated that pop-up windows are
valuable for conducting survey, commercials, and to depict
additional data while the context is intact. In addition,

people should employ pop-up windows to retain the main browser window conspicuous while exhibiting another page.

Customers often inquire analogous questions on a web site, and it can be costly and time-consuming to answer the same questions indefinitely. Organization must commence by identifying some customary inquired questions with the entire design teams. They must appraise the questions and answers in their competitor' frequently asked question pages to recognize any questions the design teams overlook. Companies must supplement their questions with those accumulated from people in close contact with target customers. They are required to employ an organizational scheme to tabulate and group related questions. Companies must append a search feature if there are any pending questions. They must utilize redundant navigation to simplify the process ensue to find the frequently asked question page on business site. In brief, companies employ the frequently asked question page merely as a transitory fix if there are usability problems. For example, the snapfish.com offers vast assistance to their customers through the company frequently asked question and answers page. This page finds solutions to entire known common questions. They are mindful of customer care and simplicity of data procurement; therefore, they arrange the questions and answers in category of the highest hierarchy of ten. Customers sometimes merit assistant from online entities in order to finalize a task. Resourceful organizations often assist their customers by inserting context-sensitive text and links in close proximity where they serve as an excellent customer care on Web page. They must seize the advantages of utilizing pop-up windows to exhibit the help segment thereby permitting people to judiciously proceed with their tasks. The site design teams must embed the context sensitive help in close proximity of the vital content. Innovative online organizations embed context-sensitive help on their site to guard against errors. The context-sensitive help will elicit consequential error communication to the customers. The site designs teams must append context-sensitive help to a precise frequently asked question or exhibit it a pop-up window to enable customers retain the context of their tasks. For example, Dell provides links to context-sensitive in order to provide customers with detailed descriptions of the features. This context-sensitive help is contained in a pop-up window, letting customers maintain the context of the task as well as observing the information they are searching for.

In order to keep customers stay focus and finalize tasks, the organization where I works eradicated the following tools, such as, (a) navigation bars, (b) tab rows, (c) irrelevant action buttons, (d) location bread crumbs and (e) embedded links. Accordingly, the organization must exact absolute site branding in order for customers to understand their locality. The site design team must now execute process funnels to avert errors and apportion *meaningful error messages* when error materializes. In brief, the organization must track customers via *persistent customer sessions* to evade predicaments with the *back button*, and to save the data that the customer inserted.

With grid layout, the limitation further includes complexity to arrange the several rival elements of a Web page, in consistent manner, without generating disorder and overwhelming the reader. The side design teams must generate a grid layout that they can employ to arrange all of the elements on a Web page. In addition, they must sketch out numerous grid layouts to perceive if they can accept the vital navigation and content elements. Accordingly, they must employ usability tests on the grid layouts of the navigation and content, and decide if customers can deduce the elements solely because of the position and layout.

In about the fold, finding depicts that customers often overlook navigation rudiments and content. This dilemma of misplace navigation and contents usually occurs when online participants engages to scroll down to observe this elements.

The organization site managers must ascertain that the most essential material is place at the top of the Web page, because this is easily visible and easily accessible. Site managers must examine the page to observe how it appears on various screen sizes and to ascertain that the vital navigation elements and content are always conspicuous.

How can a Web page be cleverly designed with a solitary unifying focus when there are several visual elements competing for attention? The design teams must employ a clear first read to provide each page a unite focal point on the most vital message. They must embed the features that emphasize the imperative element of that page. The site design teams must further utilize color, size, font, weight, and position to distinguish and accentuate the first read. They must embed lower-resolution exhibits. Finally, the online company must invite customers to assess the first reads with them; this will allow the company to evaluate for efficiency.

Many Web pages are constraint with congested navigation elements and content. Another finding is that pages decline to seize the advantage of additional space when visitors resize the browser to expand it. The solution to employ here is to design company own Web pages that embrace expanding-width screen size. The site design teams create the preceding by employing relative-width HTML tables. Moreover, design teams must retain the basic navigation elements at fixed width, and permit the center area containing the main content expand.

The problem some customers have encountered seems to be browser sizes that affect the amount of text they can observe on the screen. When online participants arrange their browsers too large, each line of text becomes too long to peruse comfortably. The design teams should utilize a fixed-width screen size to craft the long tracts of text to be more readable by limiting the width of the text column. They must generate fixed-width screen sizes by employing absolute widths in the HTML tables. The managers at CNET News.com preserves their Web site pages fixed width so that the content stays in the center of the page. The quest to discover the related content on a Web page can be frustrating for many prospective customers. The design teams are responsible for implementing consistent sidebars of related content, they shall create the location of sidebars consistent by employing a grid layout and page templates. They must determine a maximum length for sidebars in order to bring stability to the page layout. The organization must equally maintain the preceding for all visitors who may participate on online shopping spree.

Chapter 13

The search engines may rank pages higher if search terms are included in titles. The design teams must utilize keywords, those that site designers would use most frequently to explain the site's purpose and offering to customers. Design teams should position the keywords at the top of each page and in the body of the text. Design teams must include descriptive *meta* tags representative of the content contained in each page. They must make their site accessible to people with impaired vision. They must evade embedding the system with bogus keywords and text-an approach that defeat goal achievement. For examples, e-loan.com retains most of it keyword-filled content high on the homepage, which helps the company score high percentage on search engine rankings. The cancernet.org utilizes keywords in the body of the company homepage to help improve the search engine rankings. To help customers scrutinize for the most relevant site, yahoo.com search results often incorporate each keyword, as it functions in context of each site. Including keywords in context is one of the most vital strategies for improving site rankings on search engine lists and click-through. Consequently, design teams must incorporate the page title, keywords, and descriptive text to help ensure high rankings in Web search results. They must arrange the pages in the Web sites so those searches engines can find and process data more effectively, making it easier for customers to find the company site.

People fidget about quickly on the Web, skimming for information or key words. If a site's writing is not quick and easy to grasp, the audience will often refuses to peruse it. Meanwhile, the inverse-pyramid writing style is defined as a journalistic approach of writing short sentences, key words, in a straightforward manner that evades complex sentences.

The inverse-pyramid writing makes it easier for prospective customers to scan, comprehends, browse and search. The online company must commence with a concise but descriptive headline, and continue with the most important points. Similarly, the online organization will have to employ less text for print, in a simple writing style that utilizes bullets and numbered lists to emphasize information. Accordingly, the design teams must position embedded links in their text to help visitors discover more information about a related topic. The online organization will have to conduct experiment with different writing styles for entertainment reasons. For examples: a concise yet descriptive headline, an engaging blurb, simple, and obvious writing are paragon of the first paragraphs on the yahoo.com Internet life site, thus, a prime example of the inverse-pyramid writing style. The most significant paragraph in cnn.com news article is at the top and they depict this in boldface. Consequently, they let the following paragraphs prolong the story and draw readers in. The cnetbuilder.com Web page derives benefit from an inverse-pyramid style. They embed the one that has a concise title, a short synopsis paragraph, and supporting paragraphs. The benefit is that the customers do not have to peruse the supporting paragraphs in order to comprehend the essence contain in the Web page. For inverse pyramids, the design teams must start with a good title, persist with a few blurbs, and follow up with supporting information.

Occasionally, customers may want to print what is on their screen. Customers may become frustrated if a printed Web page delete content, continuously print pages of irrelevant data, or does not offer a *printer-friendly* version. The solution to the aforementioned predicament will require the design teams to construct a printer-friendly page template that removes frames; create additional columns, navigation bars, and sidebars. Resourceful design teams must term the page as the URL, author and page title. In brief, let the organization ascertain that the main content is not position within a table as this can cause serious printing problems.

For examples, marthastewart.com make it simple for their customers to print Web pages by linking them to a ingenious printable format that shred out navigation elements, frames, and advertising, leaving the logo and the content. The yahoo.com preferred to create a single-column format for its printer-friendly version. They also eliminated the sidebar of related content from the bottom of the page. To make the company site pages more printable, creative design teams simplify the situation by eradicating extra columns.

The HTML page titles are widely utilized for features, such as, browser, bookmarks, favorite and desktop shortcuts. They are widely employed by search engines when exhibiting search results. The page titles do not supply useful reminders of page contents. In order to attain a distinctive HTML titles, resourceful design teams must create distinct names for each page, even if the pages are produce from page templates. Online organizations must consider utilizing the site's organizational hierarchy as the basis for titles that explain the categories and subcategories of each page. Everyone knows that desktop shortcuts employ the HTML titles as names. The public also knows that Web browsers utilize HTML titles as the names of the bookmarks. Consequently, resourceful companies employ a different name for each page on their site.

The Web is a global medium, but several sites do not contribute language, culture and economic transaction for international and nonnative audiences. People from global scale can visit a site, but they will find the experience frustrating if language, cultural, economic transactional issues and lack of administration. The online company must store strings separately from code so that text is advance to and simply expedited by the designated translation team. In order to internationalized and localized content online company will not depend on machine translation. They must hire proficient multilingual translators. The organizations may have to manipulate internationalization, and localization processes through either a centralized or decentralized system. Meanwhile, they are cognizance that certain local verbal communication and concepts may not be widely recognized, and that holidays, customs, and nonverbal communications in other cultures can affect a site's design. Design teams shall make necessary modification on how they embody certain information, such as dates and currencies. The organization shall continue to be cognizance of the devices people use to surf Web sites because mobile customers may be a large audience for their services. They must know which legal issues might affect their business. Online organizations are infamous for providing customized services to locales that do not have the same practices as those they are addressing domestically. In brief, the Web sites market entail internationalized and localized for a worldwide audience. Finally, design teams should stockpile strings for different languages in separate files. Consumers from worldwide might visit company Web site if this company embed linguistic, cultural, and economic perspectives. Organization must redesign the site pages that will enable printer-friendly features so that the site pages will print effectively. In addition, the online manager should implement sophisticated printable format that shred out navigation elements, frames, and advertising, leaving the logo and the content.

Trust is vital to commence a relationship with customers. According to the concept, without trust and credibility, prospective customers have no reason to believe or procure products on the company Web site. The site branding often supersedes or dominate over images. As a benchmark for customers, they need to know where they are and whether they can trust the Web site to provide something vital and unique. The designer is required to build a strong site brand by differentiating the company from other companies through the promises that the company makes and through the actions the company takes to gratify customers. Design teams may want to maintain graphical elements to attune with (a) consistent in style, (b) moderate in size, (c) in the upper left corner, and (d) reusable from page to page. For example, the msn.com employs their brand very consistently throughout their site. Studies have shown that a good branding statement results from several factors. Accordingly, in all material respect, online company should make the brand the first read in the upper left corner of every page on their site. The site brand should permit prospective consumers to quickly recognize where they are on the site, cultivating a trusted and credible attribute for organizations.

The management and marketing department of the companies are responsible for maintaining contact with customers who are interested in what their site has to offer. The online companies shall make the system simple for people who are interested to set up an e-mail subscription. They shall make necessary effort to write newsletter, focused advertisements, and alerts in inverse-pyramid style. The standard is to employ text e-mail message except one knows that the recipients' personal computer software can read HTML e-mail. The design teams must incorporate information about how to subscribe and unsubscribe in each e-mail message. They must employ their customers' e-mail addresses only for consensual purposes. For examples, the networkforgood.com has a text entry field on the bottom left portion of their homepage that makes the aspect simple for people to subscribe to news about upcoming events and new Web site features. Several sites let people sign up and extend notifications to customers when major new features or when they deploy site redesigns. The yahoo.com permits people sign up for newsletters when they create an account. The amazon.com has an attribute on their search results page that informs customers when latest products matching the input search criteria materialize. Accordingly, the tveyes.com utilizes e-mail subscriptions to notify customers when any of the keywords they have elected are contain on the television broadcast. In short, the e-mail subscriptions are widely employed to send newsletters, focused commercials, and alerts to interested and self-selected customers. The online organization should employ e-mail subscriptions to

articulate and stay in touch with their visitors about new events, merchandise, and special developments.
Privacy is a serious concern for several people using the Web site. However, it is not always apparent what policies and procedures should govern a web site. The online companies employ these privacy policies to handle customer personal information in a fair and secure manner.

Chapter 14

The organization shall make necessary effort to have a clear privacy policy, and make it obvious on key Web pages. They must permit the customers to choose how their information is used. There should be provision for account management tools to let customers review and correct their personal information, such as, login name, id and password. Meanwhile, companies should protect their customers' personal information. They must provide knowledgeable guidelines for gathering, administering and using customers' personal information. Organization should possess a certification in a safe harbor Web site if they conduct business with customers or companies in European Union nations. As an example, the safe harbor Web site elicits vast information about the safe harbor privacy contract between the United States and the European Union. Safe harbor compliance is vital for companies aspiring to do business with citizens and companies in the European Union. The organizations must be proactive to create their privacy policy to elicit the followings: (a) to safeguard customers data, (b) to simplify the way customers manage their data, (c) conspicuous privacy policy, (d) to provide security against identity theft and (e) enable customers to update their information.

Many customers are apprehensive about the privacy of their dossier online. Web sites need a way of informing their customers up front about the kinds of information collected and how the company employs that information to provide value. They might even disclose the circumstances under which the company discloses consumer information to the third party. Online organization should enable the availability of confidentiality policy on each Web page. They must precisely address and incorporate the U.S. fair information practices bylaw. Management should be cognizance of special privacy policies for children and embed

the same policies on the site. Meanwhile, the U.S.
government Web sites must contain a clear and conspicuous
privacy policy. The online corporations must be mindful to
converse about special exceptions for valid legal procedures
in their privacy policies. The advantage is that this provides
tangible value for personal information. For example, the
ftc.gov web sites adheres to the bylaw by depicting privacy
policies that elucidates about what kind of information the
site accumulate and how they employ the information.
Similarly, the exploratorium.edu web sites has a concise and
simple privacy policy, describing the kind of information that
is amass, how they utilize the information, the exception
conditions, and the fact that the site refuses to request
personally identifiable information from children. In concise,
the exploratorium.edu enables the availability of privacy
bylaw on each web page of the company site.

Many Web sites have an excellent deal of valuable
background profile that is distinct from the main focus of the
Web site, such as contact information and public relations.
There is a need to arrange this information. The online
company must amass background information in *about us*
pages. These *about us* pages should assist people to learn
more about the company or site, what the site do, and why
they can trust this company. The company web site must
contain the dossier like: (a) organizational profile,
background (b) mailing addresses, map, telephone numbers
(c) disclaimers and legal information, (d) customers and
partners, and (e) employment opportunities. In addition,
organizations must also embed: (a) public relations, (b)
investor relations, (c) community relations, (d) site credits,
and (e) often-asked questions. The Google's *about us* web
page seek several customer groups, including people that
prefer to understand search engines, site owners embarking
on advertising, those enhancing their ranking in search
results, and prospective employees. For examples, the
craigslist.org has an easy, practical about us page. The
mission segment of craigslist.org explains the values and

history of the site. The press section has links to where the site receives citation in mainstream media, including a public relations kit for journals. The segment name *using the site* section recount what is acceptable behavior in the community forums. Similarly, the lego.com about us web pages contain a page about fair play, recounting why lego.com has to defend its trademarks, and the bylaw that fans may and may not comply with when creating their own web sites. The LexisNexis *about us* page comprises several of the features such as organizational profile, contact information, and disclaimers and legal information. Although the exact content for the *about us* pages will differ from site to site, they should be simply accessible from the homepage portal. In order to build trust via *about us* page, organization must embed dossier about the celebrity and fortune five hundred company embarking the e-commerce site.

People are often uncomfortable transmitting sensitive information over the web site because of privacy and security concerns. In order to secure connections organizations employ a labeled icon or a labeled action button to let customers know that they are conveying information securely. If needed, present a Web page recounting the security practices the organization use to reassure customers that the vital information that belongs to them are secure and safeguarded. For examples, the half.com contains the checkout process that they conduct over a secure connection. Half.com emphasized this fact by inserting a secure *shopping icon* at the top right of the checkout pages. Amazon.com utilizes a labeled button to let customers comprehend that the login information will be secure. Similarly, the cdnow.com provides secure connections for its shopping cart. An action button labeled *proceed to secure checkout* emphasizes the proclivity of this point. In addition to employing secure connections, llbean.com contains assurances that all orders taken on its web site will be safe and secure. The web pages should offer feedback to let customers know when the user is transmitting information securely. In short, special care should be widely taken that the secure connection is in effect for as long as necessary. The goal of the web site includes the facilitation of interactions, information access and information sharing among its millions of global participants. The site has the potential to enhance its users' access to and use of relevant commerce related data that elicit trust and credibility.

Effective use of the web site should result in a more informed, knowledgeable, trust and credibility. However, it is important to point out that use of the web site exposes organizations and the customers to web site related risks. Organizations should implement embed security bylaws and extensive effort to minimize and protect customers from all related risks. Examples include online or files that contain viruses, email viruses and unwanted intrusion into the servers network by hackers. Thus, online organizations must exercise prudence and caution in addressing security issues. Any significant connection, privacy and security problems in using web site should be resolve by the site managers and design teams.

The capability to discover and acquire products online is one of the most compelling reasons to use the Web, but for consumers to be successful, the site design must contain clean, simple interfaces and support for common task. This design should elicit customer experience on the company e-commerce. An e-commerce shopping experience may not be pleasant. A purchase might not be accomplished, if the checkout method is cumbersome, confusing, or error prone. For this reasons, the amazon.com check out often let the customer to specify what is necessary, see the vital details, and finish quickly. By the last page of the checkout process, half.com discontinues cross selling and up selling to customers primarily to guarantee that they will complete their orders. The practical solution to checkout method that is cumbersome, confusing, or error prone is the quick flow checkout system. Quick flow checkout is simple to administer all one have to do is follow a simple four-step approach so that customers can finish their orders in a secure area of the site. For examples, (a) customers can check out without storing their profiles, (b) identifier is employ so that customers do not need to reenter data, (c) they situate expectation by showing an overview of the process, and (d) they provide solutions to common questions. Online organization collects the following information: (a) shipping data (b) handling data, and (c) shipping techniques so that they can compute the total cost of the order, including taxes, at the next step. Organization discloses total cost of the order jointly with the order summary so that customers can authenticate that the information is correct. A company can request for payment information via confirmation and alleviate any concerns about the security and privacy of their customers' financial data. Company often confirms that funds for the order are currently available, and offer the customers a final chance to confirm the order. When the order is complete, company usually provide a printable receipt and invite individual customers to revisit. An example that comes in handy for solution is the use of amazon.com methods; this site often extends answers to deal breakers on key pages so that customers can have their questions answered quickly.

Similarly, they let the customer stipulate what is necessary, see the important details, and finish quickly. An excellent order confirmation page comprises an order number, the order date, shipping data, billing details and an itemized list of all products ordered. Customers can print this confirmation page and employ it for reference in future. The checking out should be a simple four-step procedure that directs customers toward completion of an order: such as, (a) shipping, (b) billing, (c) summary, and (d) confirmation. The site design teams should embed a quick, simple and reliable quick flow checkout pattern that will aid consumers to finalize a smooth purchase.

The Principles of Modern Web Design

Chapter 15

When shopping, customers desire to observe clean product details to help inform their buying decisions. They must also trust a seller prior to deciding to make a purchase. Many sites do not offer sufficient in-depth information about their products or they project an untrustworthy image. Company actualizes in-depth information in a grid layout. They maintain vital items that every customer will need above the fold, such as, (a) general navigation, (b) product thumb-nail, (c) need-based explanations, (d) prices, and (e) an options pick list. In addition, this includes (a) a link to a configuration page, (b) product ratings, (c) delivery time frame, (d) the *add to cart* action button, (e) links to more detailed data, and (f) even if the data is farther down on the page. Site designers often place secondary items, such as full product description, appraisals, related products, and a product comparator if possible, below the fold. Dell.com contains product details page that emphasizes the most vital information high on the page to make sure it appears above the fold. In-depth data appears underneath the fold and on separate tabs. The site also offers some unique features, such as the product configuration button and they *customizes it* because individual merchandise has several options. An excellent product description pages are available to incorporate the key product details, such as, the description, a thumbnail, and the price above the fold and additional data underneath the fold.

Customers often want to gather and procure several items in one transaction. Online shopping carts can offer much more that supersedes their offline competitors the benefit this technology includes the simplicity to change the quantity of an item in the shopping cart. Conversely, making shopping carts easy and useful requires self-control. Companies often provide customers with simple access to the shopping cart from every page of their site. They should enable customer to track their intending product before they finalize the purchase. On product detail page, companies often make the technology *add to cart* buttons hard to miss. On the shopping cart page itself, company frequently provides highly visible action buttons leading to checkout and action buttons to proceed to the shopping segment, along with the top-level navigation elements and search features. In the detail of the contents, companies often include (a) product name, (b) a concise explanation, (c) a link to the product page, (d) availability time frame, (e) price, quantity, (f) a button to delete each item, (g) shipping, (h) tax, and (i) subtotal data or links. The site often depicts a link to their return policy. Optionally, company might also cross-sell and up-sell other products on the cart page, and place a synopsis of the cart contents on every site page. An example that is versatile for solution is the use of amazon.com shopping cart that maintains navigation to the rest of the site obviously indicated at the top of the page, but it also formulates checking out even more abundantly clear. For a business that procures money via online via sales, it is vital that customers discover their way through to checkout. Each product page should give an obvious way to append the product to the shopping cart. One finds that amazon.com employs action buttons to make it look like customers can push down what they term as *add to shopping cart* button. Additional example of how online company can implement an excellent shopping cart is to imitate the steps of cdnow.com that permits customers to save items in a wish list, helping them to recollect the products they would like to purchase. The abovementioned strategy also makes it easy to shift items from the wish list to the shopping cart. Another example of how online company can implement a sophisticated shopping cart is to mimic the strategy of buy.com that cross-sells extra products on the shopping cart page. The empirical research discloses that these products are well known; customers generally do not need to research them and may merely click the check box to append them to their orders.

This strategy is analogous to what supermarkets do when they display magazines and candy next to the checkout stand. The cdnow.com provides shopping cart that informs customers how many items are in it. An excellent shopping cart shows customers details about their purchases, including the price tag of the order, and then makes it simple to check out without being distracted.

Inserting addresses need not be cumbersome, particularly if customers are ordering from a site for a second time. At the pinnacle of the page, companies prefer to provide a link to the vicinity where users can insert a new address. They also prefer to situate all formerly stored addresses next, with a *use this address* action button next to each one. They frequently create a new address form that is quick and easy to read: such as, (a) with labels right-aligned, (b) with left-aligned input field beside the same vertical grid line, (c) employing a minimum of fields, (d) minimum instructions, and (e) a *use this address* action button. A first illustration of how a company can offer quick address selection method is to impersonate the strategy of half.com that permits an address book to provide a simple, clean, single-column form for inserting a new address. To help people check out speedily, nordstrom.com stockpile customers' addresses for speedy reuse and offers space for a new destination. To keep the customer from forgetting the context of the order, snapfish.com utilizes a pop-up window for its address form. In brief, customers are encouraged to use addresses they have entered before, and the option is available to append new addresses easily.

Customers often resent hidden shipping and handling charges, and they desire to choose the finest shipping option for their situation. Online corporations have the advantage to embed a pick list or radio buttons for selecting shipping alternatives. They might confer a high-level narrative of the delivery time frames and the associated costs. They often compute the shipping costs on the dimension of size and the weight of the products the company will ship. According to the text book organization must provide links to more in-depth information about shipping concerns, including international requirements and insurance. An example could be a nordstrom.com web site that provides a pick list right next to the shipping details so that customers can speedily pick the finest shipping method and see how it affects the price. Customers often employ amazon.com radio buttons to choose the shipping method. Clicking on update depicts the cost of the chosen shipping method in the order summary on the right location. Another excellent idea would be to show the costs right next to the radio buttons as well. An additional example could be a buy.com web site that often provides the shipping method as a pick list item in the shopping cart, so customers can choose it along with the price. The shipping page updates customers of their options and costs for shipping, while moving them through the checkout process with little interruption. In brief, online company must enable overnight or regular surface mail shipping options to address customer convenience.

When it comes to paying for an order on site, people prefer to demand security and simplicity. The online companies must dismiss any apprehension that consumers might have about security and privacy policy by addressing them up front with a link to the site. Companies may elect to embed a pick list or radio buttons that will help customers select the billing options. They often implement a new credit card form that is quick and easy to peruse, they comprises attribute such as (a) one with labels right-aligned (b) input fields left-aligned along the similar vertical grid line, (c) utilizing a minimal of fields, (d) negligible instructions, and (e) *use this card* action button. If storing multiple billing addresses, companies may execute them above the new address form include a list of all formerly stored addresses with a designation for *use this address* action button next to each one. An example of how online company can proffer an excellent payment method is to emulate the steps of half.com techniques that often provide the expediency to employ previous billing information or quickly enter new billing data. With only a minimal of fields for the credit card details, the company can quickly duplicate the address from the shipping data. An additional example of how online company can represent an outstanding payment method is to imitate the stratagem of the billing data page contain on salesforce.com site, this concept depicts how few fields are required to process business billing. This salesforce.com performs funnel then asks whether to bill by purchase order or credit card. Whereas, amazon.com permits customers to choose credit cards and the related billing address on two pages. (a) On the first page customers may opt for a stored card or insert a promotion code. (b) On the second page, customers have the option to choose one of the current billing addresses in their amazon.com address book or insert a new one. Customers have the alternative to stipulate how to pay for their orders, whether by selecting from formerly used billing data or by inserting new data. Readers of this book, please recommend and encourage your organization to consider developing a policy that will serve as the basis for implementing site payment method. The design teams must embed a new credit card form that is quick and easy to peruse by the customers. The online managers must implement an excellent payment method by permitting customers to select prefer credit cards and the related billing address on two pages. Employing this payment process would enhance the process of dispensation of sales and procurement of revenues.

Chapter 16

When completing orders, customers often desire to observe everything related to what they are purchasing: the exact products, all the charges, and the billing procedures, as well as where, how, and approximately when packages will be delivered. If any one of these elements is absent from an order summary, customers might abandon their prospective purchases. First, through ordinary summary companies elect to let the customer recognize that the order is still yet to complete or expedite thus companies often provide high-visibility action buttons for completing the order. Second, companies demonstrate the items the individual shopper is acquiring and the entire data that the customers entered: (a) address, (b) payment process, and (c) shipping selections. The online companies also embed action buttons to amend these items in case they are incorrect. Third, the management of online companies frequently computes and present the total costs, including shipping and taxes. An example of how online company can symbolize an excellent ordinary summary is to implement the strategies that amazon.com embody, such as, a single, organized page that summarizes a complete order and embed links to correct the individual elements. However, this order summary from Nordstrom.com inform the customer that the order is not yet complete and actualizes high-visibility action buttons above and underneath the fold so that the customer will observe what to click to complete the order, even if scrolling is necessary. This page would operate better if this technology promotes the simple advantage for customers to change the shipping or billing information. For instance, once customers have inserted their billing and shipping data at snapfish.com that elicit online photo service and a summary of the order that verifies the following: (a) costs, (b) taxes, and (c) entire items. The online companies often summarize the entire data that the customer has inserted, such as, the items they are purchasing, the shipping and billing data, and price tags. In order to elicit customer satisfaction companies often make it easy for the customer to change any of this information and to observe whether the order still needs to be updated.

According to the concept of order summary, after the shoppers complete their orders, if customers do not get confirmation or a receipt that signal that the order has gone through, they will be uncertain of their order status and have to labor to find confirmation evidence. The online companies must now recognize that it indispensable to provide customers a thank-you on a printable page that also depicts: (a) the order number, (b) the order date, (c) the order data, (d) items purchased, quantities, prices, (e) shipping prices, tax, total, and (f) shipping and billing information. Customers are widely given an action button to continue shopping, and the company often cross-sell on other products the customers might be interested in purchasing. The order confirmation and thank-you page makes it apparent to the customer that the order is successful. It also depicts the date of the order, the order number, and all items in the order. They are printable page from snapfish.com. The confirmation should depict all of the product items, as well as the shipping and billing information. An order confirmation page permits customers to know that their orders have gone through. The customers usually obtain summary information to record what they bought and the details of the billing and shipping for future reference.

On occasion, items unfortunately are order accidentally, damaged during delivery or the customers just do not want it anymore. When organization permit customer to return this items as quickly and easily, customers are more likely to revisit the site and reorder. Online company must represent simple and liberal return policies. However, making return easy is not simple. The following depicts the steps online companies would negotiate to retain customers: (a) embed the return policy on entire product and checkout pages, including a link to a return process. (b) Customers may throw away a return label, confer them the ability to print another one, and (d) employ the label to track returns as they arrive. A site can help close sales by permitting customers to know that returns are not only possible, but also simple. This requires trust for customers to purchase items from web site though site owner are unseen. Knowing that they can make a mistake and escape charges, this is reassuring to customers. An example of how online company can epitomize an excellent easy return method is to imitate the strategy of buy.com that obviously underscore its return policy and provides a clear link to make a return. The standard of inserting a link to the return policy on every page helps ensure that customers know they can return items. Meanwhile, this is the primary step in educating customers about company return policy, and giving them quick access to the return process. Another example of how Web site can proffer an excellent easy return method is to imitate the strategy of amazon.com that embeds these links of easy return on every product page. In addition, the amazon.com process often asks customer if they would like to print a return label. If the customer elects to print a return label, amazon.com automatically generates this label and gives instructions on how to utilize it. Online organizations may create return process simply by actualizing process funnel that takes customers gradually through identifying the order, specifying the items to return and the reasons why, and finally printing a shipping label if necessary.

The community members desire to share ideas, views, and opinions with other likeminded individuals, whether they reside across the street or across the planet. However, a host of problem must be resolved, such as community usage policies, moderation of forums, anonymity, archives, communication, trust, sociability, growth, and sustainability. The challenge is to strike a balance within the online community. The site visitors like to chat, debate, gossip, and share stories with others. Designating a place for customers to congregate can be a powerful way of attracting people to the Web site, but only if people feel included and if the available tools provide ways to manage the discussions. To make a community conference functions well, organization should establish a clear community usage policy that stipulate behavior that are acceptable and sanctions that will be imposed on anyone who violates the rules. The standard is to set up a diversity of synchronous and asynchronous forums to suit the organization and the customers. One should determine if the community will be moderated, and if so, to what degree. Agree on the level of anonymity the community will maintain. The standard is to decide whether messages will be archived and if so how they will be archived and who will have access to them. Successful online companies enhance trust and sociability by keeping discussions on track and establishing social norms of behavior. They promote growth by leading discussions and attracting new community members. The organizations that require non-anonymous sign-ins for entrance to community conferences will enable the community members to operate more respectfully and responsibly. Online organization prefers managed discussions in order to keep conversation on target. For example, the Belief.net' community segment proffers several ways for participants to come together, which includes large open discussions, smaller closed groups, and personal groups used on special occasions for families and close friends. Meanwhile, the online community at various Web sites sets the policies for postings as soon as customers visit the list of forums. For example, anonymous postings can be vital on the Greenpeace Cyber-activist Community site, where users might want to participate in environmental activism without notifying their employers. Whereas, in the WELL's community, concurring individual can exchange ideas, develop a rapport and build strong trusting relationships. The site requires real names, confirmed identities and the outcome helps build this trust. Conversely, when the site requires non-anonymous sign-ins for entrance to community conferences, the community members will behave more respectfully and responsibly.

Managed discussions uphold conversations on desire objectives.

Creating a government agency's information available on the Web can be helpful. Whereas if the agency is too large and centrally controlled. Sometimes this Web site would be unresponsive, bureaucratic, and impersonal to its customers. Government sites are intended to serve the consumers but often lack apparent, understandable designs. Although these sites repeatedly have small budgets, it is still possible to construct valuable and effective sites that serve customers well. Organizations have duties to offer secure, autonomous self-service applications that report current process status through the site and e-mail after the primary request submission. Several online companies habitually give the customers the estimated time to complete the task, based on the kind of request made. They create personalize site information for each citizen by giving direct access to that citizen's agency representative and providing answers to questions posted by local community members. The personal pages permit customer direct audience to local agents and information. The secure autonomous applications eradicate the need for people to wait in line. For examples, the official site of Sydney, Australia, convey access to government dossier and services from the convenience of each citizen's desk, eliminating red tape, bureaucracy and frustration. The city of San Jose's site shows how e-government can be done. This has eliminated complication of obtaining a construction permit, by allowing citizens to complete the entire process online. The state of California's Web site offers several useful, though not yet usable, self-service applications. This site allows citizens to make appointments at the Department of Motor Vehicles.

The nonprofits depend on financial sponsors, volunteers, and staff members to serve the needs of a client purpose. Nonprofit sites bring together various audiences, from funders and volunteers to beneficiaries and staffers.

Although these sites often have small budgets, they can still reconstruct it to supply all of the organization's needs. However, a major benefit of the Web may become jeopardize if these groups are not assembled together in a network. At a minimum, organization should implement information that addresses the question posited by financial sponsors, volunteers, staff members and beneficiaries.

Chapter 17

To harness the authority of the Web as a network, successful company usually present people with the capability to enroll for projects in a place where all team members can coordinate, participate, and record project developments for future reference. For example, Volunteer Match utilizes the Web to assist volunteers and non-profit organizations to locate each other. Other sites permit participants to donate gifts to the organizations, manage their gifts, find local sponsors for initiatives and peruse what their district has donated. Successful Web sites carry pertinent news headlines and makes it simple for members to connect to events and discuss issues. The company Web site aggregate content and resources from vast non-profit organizations, making them conveniently available all in one place. The problem associated with the grassroots information sites includes sorting through hundreds of search results about a particular topic, which is time-consuming. The online visitor needs a guide because without a guide, visitors become dishearten and relinquish, or possibly respond on partial information.

This is the type of site where people send information on their own hobbies, interests, and political causes. Visitors to a site like this will glance for information in several ways, and the site needs to accommodate these various styles. Several organizations generate value by responding to potential questions, either by presenting content that the organization author or by conveying people to Web sites that can answer their questions. The organization homepages embraces an excellent strategy of providing a topic directory of up to 20 categories or external links. Grassroots information sites offer background or specialized information on a topic and arrange other valuable resources by tendering links to external sites. The valuable company sites must resolve the needs of many online participants but a company that refuses to stabilize these needs in proportion to the audience size will liquidate. The Web sites are widely utilized to institute a brand, supply information about products, or support products, among other things. On the company homepage, above the fold, several organizations devote 95 percent of the region and links to the visitors groups that account for 95 percent of the total visitor population, and keep the residual area and links for the visitor groups that account for the remaining 5 percent. The company employs the footer of the homepage to supply explicit links for each group, including those in the 5 percent category. They balance space for the branding against the navigation needs of the target audience. Throughout the site, several companies focus their attention on the precise roles of the customers, and employ value propositions they will understand. Include in-depth presentations and lists of information to keep visitors engaged if they desire to know more.

In the educational forums, the glitch includes bringing together (a) students, (b) parents, (c) mentors, (d) alumni and (e) educators are essential to educational sites. If no forum among these groups materializes, the students' education suffers, and so does the institution. Educational Web sites promote education by publicizing and providing access to resources for traditional brick-and-mortar schools and universities. They proffer online learning, research tools, and communities for teachers and learners. The remedy includes providing news and information for students, potential students, parents, mentors, and teachers that help coordinate offline activities such as class schedules, reading list, exam schedules, and contact and office hour information for teachers and administrators. As a component of student registration, they often assemble parent and student e-mail and telephone information for direct updates. They optionally publish curriculum as well as research for other schools and universities. An education forum is a safe area where students, parents, teachers and mentors congregate to share concerns, ideas, co-develop and share activities. For example, the Phillip Academy's Web site reveals resources that bring together parents, teachers, and alumni mentors to support student education. The designers of Carnegie Mellon University constructed clear links to information targeted for these different identified groups, such as, customers, prospective students, researchers, alumni and current students.

Arts and entertainment sites suggest new emotions and thoughts by challenging customers or by presenting them an escape. However, challenging visitors with a hard-to-use interface too early in their encounter with the Web site will turn them away. Art sites challenge their visitors. Entertainment sites stimulate and incite feelings. Both must engage customers in actions that go beyond what is customary. They offer visitors permission to play and explore, as well as learn how to uncover such locations as museums, movies, and amusement parks. On the first page or pages of the Web site, they often display a straightforward interface that describes the exhibits on the site and permits link directly to them. They include link from the introduction pages to background information pages that enlarge on the exhibits. In a separate area, online practitioner provides the actual exhibits and entertainment in whatever formats are required. Once a customer has selected an art exhibit to view or a movie to play, the interface often conform to whatever is required by the artist or work of art. This is where it is permissible to break the usual rules in order to challenge or amuse the customers. For example, PBS.org conveys a straightforward interface to audio clips; video clips, and games on the site, with guides to the varieties offline programs that the organization produces. They have user-friendly homepage and background pages that provide familiar navigation cues so that people do not get lost. The actual art exhibits; movies, audio clips, games, or other entertainments are in well-defined areas.

The Web applications are not similar to software applications that frequently arrive in a shrink-wrapped box. Web applications are services that are for sale online rather than in a store, hence, they have simple interfaces distinguished to desktop applications. These elements frequently do not have documentation in printed form. Web applications assist customers to finish an assortment of related tasks without having to install or configure a vast deal of software. Similarly, customers use Web applications dissimilarly from traditional Web sites, for example, they use them for real work, often for hours every day. The online professional extends a public site where prospective customers can preview the application, see how it will work, and sign up to try it. Once they have signed up, this give them access to their application home through a secure sign-in, and provide a menu of options for their roles. The professional utilizes standard Web interface widgets for complete cross-platform and cross-browser compatibility. The Web applications elicit effective feedback about communication and processing delays. This allows online documentation, training and support. For example, Salesforce.com is refers to as sales force automation Web application that permits salespeople to observe tracking, forecasting, and editing capabilities after they create a customer account. The First Internet Bank site permits customers to simply transfer funds between accounts, view canceled checks, and manage bill payments. The site follows Web principles, such as; enabling home banking customers to transact online activities over slow network connections. The First Internet Bank site is light on graphics and performs just fine with a 56k modem. A Web application is available for retail over the Web via detailed information pages and demonstrations. Once customers have signed up; and become recipients of secure access to their application home, they see a menu of tasks and associated online help.

Companies need employees to be more productive, but each employee has responsibilities that change over time.

Employees should not have to frequently learn entirely new computing systems to discharge their new responsibilities. The management should permit a secure area customized for each employee, where the employee can visit to see a list of applications and information. Several companies employ intranets to improve communications, streamline workflow, provide a community, and enhance productivity. The organization often list employees' current or pending request of others and any pending requests made of them. The technology automatically triggers new requests via an application workflow. This support employee learning by using consistent terminology across the intranet and by devising consistent interfaces for the company Web application. If presented with customized catalog of applications and information, employees have the freedom from unnecessary items they will never use. Meanwhile, applications that activate requests also forward a request automatically to the next individual in the workflow.

This author knows that improving the performance of site genre patterns of the Web site is indispensable to longevity and survival of online businesses. Thus, every organizations must apply and embed the solutions in Pattern Group F-Basic E-Commerce. The design teams should be proficient in constructing an UP-FRONT VALUE PROPOSITION (C2) on the HOMEPAGE PORTAL (CI), and have capability to provide clear links for everyone for SITE ACCESSIBILITY (B9). The design teams and the site managers should have the capability to implement the following site genre patterns: (a) extends to customers MULTIPLE WAYS TO NAVIGATE (BI), and (b) make sure the site have BROWSE-ABLE CONTENT (B2). In addition, they should be able to (a) provide CLEAN PRODUCT DETAILS (F2) so that consumer can compare different offers, (b) pick the products or services they desire by inserting them in their SHOPPING CART (F3), (c) move through the site QUICK-FLOW CHECKOUT (FI), and (d) if essential, seize the advantage of EASY RETURNS (F9). On the site, the organization should implement a FREQUENTLY ASKED QUESTIONS (H7) page that answers ordinary questions about security, privacy, shipping, and returns. Organization should build trust by making the PRIVACY POLICY (E4) always accessible and using FAIR INFORMATION PRACTICES (G3) throughout the company. This organization desire to add daily FEATURED PRODUCTS (GI) to keep customers coming back for a glance of what the reviewers recommend, and to show them something they may not have seen before.

Chapter 18

Customers are everyday people they like to save time, and sometimes they buy more than one thing. Thus, organization must assist people to save time, and perhaps show them something they might want but have not seen, by CROSS-SELLING AND UP-SELLING (G2). Shoppers like to hear recommendations from others they trust, but they do not want to be categorized as a particular kind of person. Thus, the organization must employ PERSONALIZED RECOMMENDATIONS (G3); they can offer ideas based on what they know someone might be looking for, without resorting to a prescribed recommendation. Customers prefer assisting others, too. Accordingly, this organization will proffer a RECOMMENDATION COMMUNITY (G4), this allow customers on the site to make their own recommendations. Customers who are GIFT GIVING (G6), desires to send gifts to people in many places. Thus, in the company where I am employ, the design teams must implement MULTIPLE DESTINATIONS (G5), so that customers can purchase and send all the gifts in one order. The organization needs this because customers desire to review their orders to ascertain the products they ordered arrived. In addition, if a product that has shipped does not reach the destination when it should, the ORDER TRACKING AND HISTORY (G7) feature helps customers resolve shipping problems.

Customers navigate Web sites in various ways. If any of the key navigation tools are hard to locate or missing, visitors will find the site tedious to use. Customers navigate Web sites in several ways, so an organization need multiple, and sometimes redundant ways of navigating. One of the difficulties of Web design over traditional human-computer interface design is that on the Web, customers approach to a site in many different ways, and they come not only to the company homepage. Their objectives and tasks are often disparate.

A key to a gratifying customer experience is to sustain these differences. To ensure that the visitors complete their goals, several sites designer put the search and browse navigation tools at the top and start of the page. They put the next-step navigation tools toward the top, but opposite the start, as well as at the bottom. They constantly include navigation tools that relate and promote, so that customers find things they might otherwise miss, but the common strategy is to put these tools farther down the page. For example, Amazon.com recognizes that both intent and desire are navigation motivators. Customers can search for what they intend to buy, using browsing and searching tools. The site also supplies links to impulse items that customers might not have anticipated to buy but they finalize the purchase anyway. Two kinds of motivation embolden customers to act: intention and impulse. The customers' histories and attitudes form their objectives and triggers, from which they exercise action and assess their satisfaction. This knowledge feeds back into their histories to start the loop all over again. The navigation option at the top of several homepages supplies customers' account information in the location often term as my account. There are multiple ways to conduct search. The navigation alternatives on the left side are often available on several homepages, this style permit customers to choose from and browse through multiple shopping categories. The main content area depicts the hottest sellers, providing images and links for more details as well as links to buy the items right on the spot. By assigning the visitors multiple ways to navigate on the site, depending on their goals and desires, company can keep site participants engaged.

The browsing content on a site can be complex if the information is not recognized, or if there are no obvious and consistent navigation cues for locating content and returning to it later. Organizing company information in an apparent, constant, and useful manner can significantly simplify the customer's task of finding information. One should organize the content in several ways, in categories that make sense to the customers and in the intuitive ways they think about doing their tasks.

Practitioners should build navigation tools and cues that permit customers to know where they are, where they can go, and how to get back. The practitioners often build each page with its own reading hierarchy so that customers can scan it quickly. For example, Wal-Mart's site bestows customers with easy navigation and obvious signals for finding their way back. They can click on the Wal-Mart logo to revisit the homepage, on the tab row at the top or the navigation bar on the left to visit another section or on the location breadcrumbs near the top to backtrack. In another example, the data on the Knot's Web site is widely prearranged; clearly and aligned in a clean grid layout. The navigation bar consists of a tab row along the top and links along the left hand side, making it simple to navigate through site. The site designer should embed content in a straightforward, scan-able format that guides browsing readers from one page to the next, while giving them lucid navigation markers to make their way back.

Organizing information in a hierarchy of categories can assist customers find things. Building an effective hierarchy is not effortless. Build a hierarchy of categories with contribution from customers or from practitioners known for excellent communication skills in the subject area. Use descriptive category names that are peculiar from one another. Use techniques such as card sorting to create the categories and labels, and use strategies like group identification and category description to test. Replicate the items in multiple categories where it makes sense. Keep the maximum number of subcategories per group to between 20 and 50, and practitioners should avoid generic terms like miscellaneous. For example, Yahoo utilizes hierarchies chart to categorize thousands of Web sites. This site consist the followings: (a) art, (b) humanities, (c) society and (d) culture. Customers need assistant when browsing via large amounts of information. Online Organization should emulate FindLaw that employ hierarchy to categorize legal information, providing links to top level categories, as well as examples within each category. They should use the words that are recognizable to their customers without congesting a single category with several subcategories. Implementing multiple tasks on a site is not fast and easy unless designers connect related tasks together.

The customers tasks are widely employ as the basis for grouping and connecting related information together. The solution is to study customers, the tasks they do, and the sequence in which they accomplish the tasks. Then fabricate relationships between tasks and connect them together so that the completion of one task can immediately precede the start of the next. Site designer should link the conclusion of one group of tasks to the commencement of the next related task or tasks. There are several designers that depicts related task-based on the Web site, for example, Yahoo exemplify how combining related tasks together can make a site faster and more useful. The following related tasks congregate together: (a) coffee, (b) houses, and (c) theaters. These aforementioned tasks are only a click away from a restaurant listing, allowing planning a night out on the city easier. The site visitor clicks on a task topic on sales.force.com this offers people with space to enter update information and schedule a follow-up task. Alphabetizing a list seems like an understandable way to organize content. Long alphabetical lists on a Web site, however, are cumbersome to integrate. Practitioners should embed links to each letter group at the top of the single alphabetical list page of well-known items. As an example, a Web page with the complete alphabetical list performs best when it has links at the top to jump to each individual letter group.

Chronologically organizing content on a site assist visitors comprehend the order of content in time, whether past or future. But very long lists of events are problematic to read and use. Practitioners should display chronological lists in a vertical, horizontal, or calendar format, keeping the total number of items in each list under 50 by dividing the list into smaller groups of time. For example, a company may organize the site content into micro groups of time that permits reading about each era in a much easier dimension.

Meanwhile, in the popularity-based organization, for example, the billboard.com depicts to customers the top music hits, from top selling CDs to singles and airplays. Customers can also observe top hits by music genres, as well as by number of hits on the Web site. Customers may sometimes desire to seek out what other customers like best on company site. Some customers want to scrutinize which content or products are the most popular. However, without clear labels of how the company rated the content, over what period, popularity lists are useless. Thus, designer should build the company lists of popular content from customer usage, customer ratings, or acquired outside lists. They should label each list with a descriptive title that specifies what the company rated and over what period. The essence here includes company demonstrating the most popular content, but one must ensure to graphically label how this attains the rating and to show the time period that the ratings cover. For example, the Lycos 50 Daily Report depicts visitors the 50 most popular customer search subjects on its search engine. Accordingly, Yahoo contains a popularity-based news Web page that demonstrates the most popular stories, photographs and according to the number of times they were recipient of e-mail by customers. There is availability of IFILM's homepage for customer enjoyment and this page often shows an easily read list of the most popular short films. For instance, the ALT characteristic on the Weather Channel's site often exhibits a tool tip when a customer repositions the mouse over the image. This attribute is also valuable for people who are blind because their screen readers can read out the description of the image. Another benefit of the ALT feature is that this element depicts if the image refuses to display.

Chapter 19

As customers navigate through a site, if they fail to introduce category sections via a constant layout, each section may appear like a new site. Web sites need to convey sections of information in discrete ways, to distinguish each section from others. In addition, these sections must also maintain some resemblance so that customers know they are still on the same site. The online organization utilizes a section category layout consistently throughout the site, with the similar navigation elements, giving customers a strong logic that they are in a new section and an obvious idea of how to get back. Martha Stewart's Web site contains categories labeled well and laid out constantly. When participants travel deeper down the levels, they know where they are by the color scheme, the navigation elements, and the content. For example, constantly colored categories and banner title show Amazon.com customers that no matter which segment they are located; they are still on the same site. Organization should concentrate category pages on the featured content, while employing consistent navigation. The finding is that people with audio, visual, motor, or cognitive disabilities find it difficult to use Web sites that are not widely designed with this individual accessibility in mind. In designing the Web site, designers should keep in mind accessibility for people with audio, visual, motor, and cognitive disabilities. They should make the navigation and content both understandable and usable by employing good layout, clean visual design, straightforward text descriptions for all images and links, and alternative text-based formats for rich multimedia. They should employ features built into HTML that simplify accessibility. People that suffer from audio, visual, or cognitive disabilities can be prospective customers, but not if they find it complex to use the Web site. A rising number of people now use small Internet-enabled devices to access Web sites, and they may suffer frustration from poor usability.

The company can assist both of these audiences by designing the site with accessibility in mind. For example, the Web sites are widely designed for access and use of everyone regardless of physical capacity or computer capability. This kind of element will show a screen shot from the text-based Lynx Web browser, which provides a flavor of what the Web is like for people who are blind. When the practitioner enables the company site to permit accessibility to people with disabilities this will make the site more accessible to everyone. For instance, Microsoft utilizes a simple organizational system, excellent link labels, and understandable text labels for all of its images making it easier for customers with disabilities to access its Web pages.

In a recent department meeting, I was able to convince the management and design teams to provide customers with the multiple ways to navigate by consistently using intention based navigation. For example, the design teams are now convinced to, (a) place a SEARCH ACTION MODULE (J1), (b) link to the STRAIGHTFORWARD SEARCH FORMS (J2) at the top of every page, (c) implement a consistent NAVIGATION BAR (K2) on every page, and (d) execute BROWSE-ABLE CONTENT (B2). In the company where I work, design teams now agree to make it easier for everyone to navigate the company site with SITE ACCESSIBILITY (B9). They also concur to assist customers complete their tasks by using ACTION BUTIONS (K4) and links to CONTEXT-SENSITIVE HELP (HI) situated at the top right of the page. The design teams also agree to embed a PROCESS FUNNEL (HI) for tasks where completion is absolutely necessary. They will now implement impulse-driven navigation capability by embedding CONSISTENT SIDE-BARS OF RELATED CONTENT (16) and promotions that employ DESCRIPTIVE, LONGER LINK NAMES (K9).

The site managers, design teams and management will

implement excellent organizational schemes for the site content by using HIERARCHICAL ORGANIZATION (B3), TASK-BASED ORGANIZATION (B4), ALPHABETICAL ORGANIZATION (B5), CHRONOLOGICAL ORGANIZATION (B6), and POPULARITY-BASED ORGANIZATION (B7) separately or in combination. In the organization where I am currently an employee, design teams are known to implement CATEGORY PAGES (B8) as directories to content in subcategories. Design teams make it easier for everyone to navigate the site with SITE ACCESSIBILITY (B9). My organization is now cognizance of the strategies of allocating customers plenty opportunity to find their way back, by employing NAVIGATION BARS (K2), TAB ROWS (K3), SITE BRANDING (K6), and LOCATION BREAD CRUMBS (K6). On every page, design team will now make the content browse-able by building a hierarchy of content with a clean GRID LAYOUT (11), CLEAR FIRST READS (13), and clearly defined areas with CONTENT MODULES (D2).

The homepage is the most visited page; thus, the related design deserves serious attention so that it can contain the rich diversity of customers and their needs. Organization should enable a powerful homepage to fit the needs of the customers. Homepages have to equalize many issues, from branding to navigation to content to the capability to download quickly. The infamous homepage portal is indispensable and use by almost every site and site genre. A homepage must satisfy the needs of all prospective and existing customers by creating the company's identity, while providing MULTIPLE WAYS TO NAVIGATE (BI). This pattern develops the core for homepage designs. The homepage is the highly visited page on any Web site; thus, this design deserves exceptional attention so that it can embrace the rich diversity of customers and their needs. The organization should describe how to design a powerful homepage to fit the needs of their customers.

Homepages are term as the portal through which most online users pass. They must lure online visitors while concurrently balancing several concerns, including branding, navigation, content, and the ability to download quickly. The homepage is frequently the primary thing customers observe on organization site. This page is significant because not only is it seen 10 to 1,000+ times more than any other page, but it must also offer an excellent customer experience to seduce prospective customers to continue. The space on the page, chiefly above the fold, is limited. This must be divided between the following goals: generating the right look and feel, constructing site brand and identity, providing valuable content, making navigation easy to use, establishing a unified and logical page layout, and delivering high performance.

Designers should work hard to create a seductive page, while striking a balance with all these elements that requires iterating and refining the page through testing. This project also requires that the organization focus on building trust and providing value and options to their target customer. The text encourages the organization to build Site that epitomizes identity and brand. Customers need to know that the organization site holds a valuable promise. They also need to know it is a promise they can trust the organization to fulfill. In addition, if the site is valuable, customers will want to remember it for later, to use for themselves or to tell friends about the site. This is what it means to construct a positive identity and a valuable brand. Constructing a site brand requires denoting a promise of what the site offers, with the goal of attracting customers to come in, and earning their trust and respect by continually fulfilling that promise.

The online organizations should focus on the company's UP-FRONT VALUE PROPOSITION (C2), SITE BRANDING (EI), and PRIVACY POUCIES (E4) by using text, logos, photos, and illustrations to communicate that the online organizations are trustworthy, ethical and professional. Accordingly, the site itself must strengthen the brand by fulfilling the promise and building trust on every page. Online organizations should make a positive first impression with the right look and feel. Some visitors may dislike and abscond by style alone, or by a homepage look and feel, while the customers say, this site is not for me. Whether a site uses inappropriate colors and graphics, or the writing is unfamiliar or grating, customers respond with a refusal to a style that is not widely targeted for them. For example, Neon green screaming graphics and a skateboarding illustration might appeal to teens, but if organization employs it to represent a serious family issue or a conservative business, visitors will immediately question if they have come to the right place.

When organizations design for their target customers, they will get a positive response to the look and feel. The organization should transform the site by showing it frequently to a dozen or more members of the organization intended audience. They should conduct further testing to determine how useful the customers perceive it to be, as well as how usable it is. Although vast time is consume to conduct tests, evading early feedback will cost more in the future when the organization have to redesign the site because it is not functioning. Several organizations entice customers with site content. Each customer formulates a judgment within just a few seconds of accessing a site. This is the time organizations have to get the visitor's attention and keep it. Lively script and visuals are essential because this will transport convincing and timely content to the front page. This content often lists news, enticing imagery, seductive navigation text, and/or personalization. Designers should organize content into headlines, summaries, and body. They should entice visitors with a catchy HEADLINE AND BLURB (D3), and follow via the article page with the content body. They should make organization design cost-effective, by establishing a publishing system that can help to update and rotate CONTENT MODULES (D2) automatically. Several commercial tools make this easier to do for larger Web sites.

The text encourages the online organization to personalize content if possible. The Online visitors appreciate coming to a site customized to their desires because it makes the site feel more useful, quicker to use, and more personal. Consequently, customers feel more important and their morale increases. However, a personalized site necessitates additional effort for visitors to use. This is particularly true if customers are required to enter personalization information to utilize the site at all.

Chapter 20

Personalized sites, also known as customized sites, are also more complex to design and develop, and they entail more Web server and database resources, not to mention support for logins or cookies. If the content is diverse enough, personalization can assist customers to find what they care about and use the site more effectively. A personalized homepage will comprise CONTENT MODULES (D2) and employ PERSONALIZED CONTENT (D4) to adapt the homepage to individual customers. In order to provide this personal information, visitors need to trust organization enough to directly or indirectly convey their desires and requests. Organization must use the information the customers provide ethically, for their benefit only, and customers must trust that organization will do so. The organization should balance space for brand against space for navigation. There is a trade-off between space used for conveying the site's value and differentiation, and space used for extending customers navigation tools to find what they seek.

One should be cognizant that the first read on the homepage is often the SITE BRANDING (El) located in the top left corner, and the second read is the UP-FRONT VALUE PROPOSITION (C2), both elements must be instantly clear to customers. If these elements are not clear to customers they may become doubtful, confused, or aggravated enough to go elsewhere. Organization should let team focus on designing these two elements well, rather than using more space on the homepage for branding. Customers like to skim when they read on the Web, and they will skim any organizational homepage. Customers are always looking for concise phrases and links they recognize or deem potentially valuable. The standard for organization is to focus their design on the finding the proper wording for these phrases, and on making them easy to skim. The organization should ensure that they are employing DESCRIPTIVE, LONGER UNK NAMES (K9).

Every main audience is really composed of many subgroups, and each subgroup needs answers to its precise questions. For instance, if the main audience comprises of investors, organization must answer the inquiries of both institutional investors and direct investors. An excellent idea that comes to play is to dedicate 95 percent of the areas and link above the fold to the primary audience. One may want to keep the remaining area and links for secondary groups. If the primary audience is a products and services purchaser, answer the questions of the decision maker, recommender, and technical reviewer. Organizations often prefer to take these customers to a subsidiary page where they can select their role to obtain more targeted information.

The organizations are required to make navigation easy to use. The only way people can find their way around a site is by comprehending the navigation. This means that all levels of visitors with varying degrees of computer skills, domain proficiency, and experience with the organization Web site must quickly comprehend how to get around. The text encourages the organization to give customers MULTIPLE WAYS TO NAVIGATE (B1) so that each customer has a way that fits his or her previous Web experience. There are two necessary rules to navigation. First, people recognize that some things on a Web page can be clicked on. The organizations often avoid making customers guess what is clickable and what is not. Second, people know that when they click on something, an action will ensue. The organizations make those site actions clear and predictable. The organizations usually provide a cohesive and logical page layout because a disorganized page layout can confuse site visitors. The customers need to be able to recognize the most important objects to view instantly so that they know they are in the right place. The organizations generate a homepage that makes it easy to understand what the Web site is about and where things are located. The organizations execute a clean GRID LAYOUT (II) in a PAGE TEMPLATE (D 1) that organizes the entire page cohesively. The organizations should apply the CLEAR FIRST READS (B) pattern. The first read, a concept from graphic design, is the single component that pulls the Web page together. According to many scholars, enclosing a first read on the homepage helps give customers a place for their eyes to go first, and it provides a design focus for the page.

Organization should embed the most significant navigation tools and content ABOVE THE FOLD (12), making them visible so that the customer will not have to scroll down. Consumers do not always recognize that they can scroll down for more information, and they might overlook on things you want them to perceive right away if those things are below the fold. Make the Homepage Download Quickly. You know all about this. You go to a new site, and it takes so long to load the homepage that you back out to another site. Appraise your Web site to confirm that your homepage does not take more than a few seconds to download and appear in a browser. Here are some strategies for faster downloads: The images on your homepage are surety to be the slowest the first time a shopper navigates to your site because at that point the images are not cached yet. To capture this problem, seize the advantage of HTML POWER (I4) and use text as much as possible instead of graphics. HTML text is the first thing that downloads, so the shopper will gets all the vital text information without waiting for image downloads.

The customers often articulate that HTML text is unattractive. Organization can make the best of it by working with a Web-savvy graphic artist who can shift the site to the next design level. This design professional can designate the right complementary font colors, background colors, and font styles; make an exhilarating and dynamic homepage design. Several organization employ FAST-DOWNLOADING IMAGES (L2) to improve the velocity of their site. In addition, the study encourages organization to crop, shrink, reduce colors, and increase compression to make images smaller and faster to download.

Several companies utilize SEPARATE TABLES (L3) for page layout instead of one large HTML table. The difficulty with using a single large table is that it compels customers to tarry until all of the images are loaded before they can observe anything. If organization separates their Web page into multiple tables, people can observe some parts of the page as it is loading. On the main homepage several organizations evade slow-loading content such as sounds, splash screens, Flash animations, and Java applets. If organization includes features such as aforementioned, the main homepage will become slower to load, and also a dilemma to visitors who do not have the latest technologies installed on their computers.

On the homepage portal, one should establish and reinforce the value of the site with a strong, clearly stated promise that is executed on every page of the site. Several organizations devote 95 percent of the area and links above the fold to the visitor groups that comprise 95 percent of the total visitor population. They keep the remaining area and links for visitor groups that make up the remaining 5 percent. They use additional links in the footer of the homepage to make explicit links for each group, including those in the 5 percent category. Organization should build a homepage layout that provides strong cues to define navigation and content, and that downloads quickly. The usual standard is to test organization homepage design to confirm that they have created the right look and feel-one that attract visitors with content, regardless of whether it is personalized.

On the homepage, organization may want to clearly state the site's UP-FRONT VALUE PROPOSITION (C2), demonstrate the SITE BRANDING (EI), and grant links to the site's PRIVACY POLICIES (E4). Several organizations use a publishing system to automatically update and rotate CONTENT MODULES (D2) on the homepage. A personalized homepage will embrace CONTENT MODULES (D2) and employ PERSONALIZED CONTENT (D4) to adapt the homepage to individuals. The practitioners often make navigation easier by creating consistent MULTIPLE WAYS TO NAVIGATE (BI) and by instituting the navigation design on the homepage. Several organizations produce BROWSE-ABLE CONTENT (B2) and use NAVIGATION BARS, OBVIOUS LINKS (KIO), ACTION BUTTONS (K4), DESCRIPTIVE, LONGER LINK NAMES (K9), and EMBEDDED LINKS (K7). The online professional prefers to generate an easy-to-read homepage employing a PAGE TEMPLATE and GRID LAYOUT (II) with CLEAR FIRST READS (B). The standard is to put the most important navigation and content ABOVE THE FOLD (12). Several organizations prefer to use FAST-DOWNLOADING IMAGES (L2) and SEPARATE TABLES (L3) to enhance both the actual and the perceived performance of their homepage.

The HOMEPAGE PORTAL (CI) must articulate the reason of the site immediately and clearly. The up-front value proposition is a pattern that describes how to develop the message sites, people should be able tell when they arrive on site what the site offers. There are problems on several Web sites; such as, people often cannot know what the company or site offers. When customers come to the site for the first time and they do not observe a clear, convincing promise about what the company or site has to offer, they must figure it out on their own. Sometimes customers will leave the site because they cannot be bothered or they do not have time. Customers surf around the particular site to find the answer, and sometimes they never do understand the site or company's full value, even if the organization has stated it on the homepage.

If there is any atom of miscommunication this can lead customers to undervalue the site and the entire organization, in their critical first moments of using a site. Changing a customer's original impression later can cost organization ample money and time because organization will have to earn their trust in order to reeducate customers. Even if an organization get it right, a value proposition alone is not sufficient to make a site valuable.

Chapter 21

Organizations must fulfill their promise on every page and emphasize it offline through the business practices. A convincing value proposition, along with these other elements, will create optimistic impression with customers. This in turn will build trust and goodwill that organization can enhance and build on over time. This pattern concentrates on offering organization a proven way to communicate a powerful promise. To get there, organization should work through several ideas and iterations until an organization create the strongest statement possible.

The homepage is an advertisement for the rest of the business Web site. It must convince customers on continuing their expedition to explore, use, possibly purchase, repurchase, and revisit repeatedly. For a Web site, that means consumers are more likely to navigate and use your site. Online managers should construct s persuasive promise and a unique offering. Consumers want to observe a descriptive wording and images that are easily and quickly understood. Creating a convincing and unique statement about what your organization provides can be problematic without the right processes, people, and tools.

To write and select the best promise, use inventiveness and brainstorming exercises to pull together an initial list of candidates. You can also use customer research to construct your promise; it has been proven to help select the most convincing offer. Construct an initial list of value propositions. Invite everyone on the site design team to a brainstorming session, especially the most visionary, imaginative, and vocal members of the team. Seat everyone in a comfortable space that has a whiteboard on the wall.

Online developers please write down all suggestions, even if you do not appreciate them, they are lengthier than your target number of words, or they are not as exclusive or convincing as you would like. Continue for half an hour or more, if time permits. Then copy all the notions on a piece of paper or onto a computer for later evaluation, this is not the final step. In a brainstorming session, no one stipulates judgment. Every statement is equally important, and no statement is wrong.

The concept even encourages company to select the strongest candidates for brainstorming session. They encourage distributing the list developed in the brainstorming session to a core group of marketing and business visionaries on the site design team. Organization should ask them to identify the ten most convincingly articulated value propositions that make a unique offer. They should tell them to be prepared to support their choices. They should convene a meeting to select the ten best promises. In order to determine the best, these are the questions to ask: Is this promise consistent with organization strategic direction? Is it convincing? Is it unique? If not? Why not? Alternatively, can it be improved upon? This conference could easily take longer than the initial brainstorming session, so limit the time to a couple of hours to make the procedure manageable.

The organization value proposition is a site commercial that must convincingly articulate the company's uniqueness. Several organizations use team brainstorming to develop ideas, and improve the best ideas into a list of top ten candidates. To determine the preeminent value proposition, the primary text stipulated that one should ask customers to rate each promise on importance and uniqueness. Organizations should place the value proposition next to their homepage's logo for speedy scanning and utmost exposure. On various Web sites, people frequently cannot tell when they arrived, what the company or site offers. One thing is critical the Web sites must convey a strong message about the value they provide.

This author encourages his organization to execute the following design strategies on the homepage, for example, the design teams and site managers must clearly create the site's UP-FRONT VALUE PROPOSITION (C2), generate the SITE BRANDING (E I), and embed links to the site's PRIVACY POLICIES (E4). In the company where I work, the design teams were encouraged to employ a publishing system to automatically update and rotate CONTENT MODULES (D2) on the homepage. They must administer a personalized homepage that contain CONTENT MODULES (D2) and use PERSONALIZED CONTENT (D4) to customize the homepage to individuals. The design teams will make navigation easier by generating reliable MULTIPLE WAYS TO NAVIGATE (BI) and by establishing the navigation design on the homepage. In the organization where I work, design teams and site managers must implement (a) BROWSE-ABLE CONTENT (B2) and employ NAVIGATION BARS (K2), (b) OBVIOUS LINKS (K10), (c) ACTION BUTTONS (K4), (d) DESCRIPTIVE, (e) LONGER LINK NAMES (K9), and (f) EMBEDDED LINKS (K7). My organization must create an easy-to-read homepage utilizing a PAGE TEMPLATE (DI) and GRID LAYOUT (I1) with CLEAR FIRST READS (13). The design teams and site managers must embed the most important navigation and content ABOVE THE FOLD (12). They must implement FAST-DOWNLOADING IMAGES (L2) and SEPARATE TABLES (L3) to enhance both the actual and the apparent performance of the homepage.

Meanwhile, another approach to achieving organizational design goals is to compare two dissimilar prototypes to observe which one works best. One might find that with successful designs, customers are twenty percent faster on average than with the other design. A similar approach to attain design goal is to compare and contrast the new site design to the existing design or the design of one of the organizational competitors. Alternatively, the management of the organization might want to know how quickly customers are perfect using the sites. Discovery of this can be harder than it sounds. One could measure how many hours of use that the customers require on an average to complete tasks successfully. Otherwise, one could quantify how many task customers complete in a definite amount of time. There are several ways to implement the measurement methodologies that are vital in comparing organizational site designs against competitors. Another procedure is to measure, compare and contrast the average number of errors available on each site. When customers commit errors and become confused, they are distracted from buy products from the organizational Web sites. In order to measure errors the organization should define them. Is it an error when a person clicks on the browser's Back button? For example, let assume that the customer is procuring five cartridges of printer toner online. As he/she finishes the checkout process and fills out a form with his/she credit card number and address, he/she notices he/she forgot to alter the quantity on the order form on the previous page. The customer has to return to fill it in and then when he/she goes forward the billing information might be lost. Is this an error? Probably, you have to define what you are measuring.

Sometimes organization can look at specific pieces of their site that do not necessarily indicate an interface problem but might indicate a general problem with the content or policies. For instance, many sites evaluate the rate of shopping cart abandonment before checkout. Customers might abandon their shopping carts if they cannot locate all the products they want to purchase. Otherwise, the checkout process might be too long but design teams can solve this problem in QUICK-FLOW CHECKOUT (FI). Another reason confirms that when the organization prices are higher than a competitor's prices customer will abandon the shopping cart or people are just on the site to comparison shop. A fourth reason could be that customers are surprised about the high cost of the sales tax or shipping and handling costs are, then customers decide to abscond. At any rate, the abandoned-shopping cart metric is widely related to the organization business's revenue numbers.

The solution to any of the numerical measurements is the incorporation of statistics into research design and also to make sure that the design teams presents numbers that are reliable and valid. The organization might also want to look at more subjective metrics. An organization should let customers find the Web site more pleasing, fun and satisfying than the last version of the site, or the competitor' sites. The responsibilities of a proactive organization should include measuring responses to questions on an ongoing basis to understand how their site and the customer' opinion change over time. This information will help organization to recognize when they need to conduct more in-depth research. Again, some organization relates these numbers directly to their bottom-line revenue or profit. Some sectors advocate that an excellent idea for an organization to embark upon is to measure these subjective issues with surveys. Online surveys are simple to create. They represent sample survey of the customers that the designers embed one of the Web pages. An excellent idea is to target additional surveys for specific pages or for times when customers take specific actions. An organization may ask visitors why they abandoned their shopping carts. Several organizations perform customer survey, right when it happens.

The design goals we have communicated about so far are only an approximation of the higher-level client and business goals. For example, shorter task completion time and fewer abandoned shopping carts are imperative metrics to work toward, but the business goal for an e-commerce site is to maximize revenue. The problem is that expert simply cannot collect this kind of metric using prototypes. Still, prototypes are good enough to deliver useful feedback that will bring practitioner closer to the overall goals. Design goals signify the destination an organization wants to reach after design teams complete the building of a Web site. Design principles will channel organizations to that destination. The following individual provided regulation for interface design: for instance, (a) Ben Shneiderman advanced eight golden rules for interface design, (b) Jakob Nielsen presented ten heuristics, and (c) Edward then explained something on information presentation.

Chapter 22

In interface design, an organization should utilized consistent succession of actions to complete analogous tasks. The Web pages should contain consistent color, layout and fonts. For instance, the NAVIGATION BAR (K2) are widely embedded in the same place on every page, and ACTION BUTTONS (K4) that accomplishes exact activities appears in the same general location across dissimilar parts of the site. Design team should utilize equal terms in diverse places across the site. Designers should make Web site consistent with the real world, for example, they should follow real-world conventions, and use FAMILIAR LANGUAGE (KII) by using expressions that all customers will understand, and they should avoid technical terminology. They should present informative feedback. The design teams should depict the status of the system visible, and keep the customers knowledgeable about what is going on. For example, this is the theory behind SECURE CONNECTIONS (K4), which permits customers to know whether the information they are sending over the Internet will be safe. The designer teams should depend on recognition over recall. Short-term memory is the key inadequacy in human cognition. They can minimize the short-term memory load by permitting customers to recognize what they need to identify from visible objects, actions, options, and directions.

On occasion, the memory load is unfortunately much higher if they need to remember this information from memory with no visual aids. This is the reason a visual human-computer interface such as the Macintosh or Windows is easier to study than a command language-based interface like DOS. This is the reason ACTION BUTIONS (K4) always contains a textual label to go along with the graphical icon.

The optimum responsibilities of an organization is to assist customers prevent and recover from errors, because errors cause frustration, poor performance, and a lack of trust on the site. The concept of PREVENTING ERRORS (K12) will help online organization to avoid many of these problems. Unfortunately, no matter how well online organizations design the site; humans are prone to make occasional errors. In other to assist people recuperate from errors by presenting MEANINGFUL ERROR MESSAGES (K13). Inform them what happened and how to mend, or better yet, offer to automatically bring out the steps that would assist them mend from the error. Support customer control and freedom. Customers should perceive that their actions govern the site's responses, and that they are not being forced down a fixed path. Providing MULTIPLE WAYS TO NAVIGATE (B1) is one example of how to support this attitude on your site. It also means that the customer is given stress-free exits, such as undo and redo, for mistaken choices. The browser's built-in Back and Forward buttons and LOCATION BREAD CRUMBS (K6) are both mechanisms that give customers stress-free exits on the Web. Help frequent customers utilize accelerators. Keyboard shortcuts are imperative for expert customers. Your site can support recurrent actions automatically. For example, your site can accumulate information such as shipping addresses so that your customers do not have to retype this information every time they navigate to that page. Design an ACCOUNT MANAGEMENT (H4) interface that makes it user-friendly for your customer to perceive and change this accumulated information. Strive for aesthetic and minimalist design. Clean aesthetics make navigating your site a pleasing experience. A GRID LAYOUT (11) is one collective technique you can utilize to ensure that your site has a clean, understandable appearance. Well-designed type, images, and graphical elements communicate how the site works. Often visual components are overused. If removal does no damage to the site, eradicate irrelevant information and graphics from all pages. Avoid embedding extra elements because every extra element on the website draws attention away from the ones that matter.

In general, early in the design phase and prototyping stages design teams develop three kinds of design relics, such as, site maps, storyboards, and schematics. A site map is a sophisticated diagram presenting the overall structure of a site. The practitioner employ prototype mainly to replicate an understanding of the information configuration or architecture of the site during the construction to a limited extent, the navigation structure, and flow through the site. A storyboard is a series of Web pages representing how a customer would achieve a given task. Online design teams implement storyboards to indicate important interaction series, or flows through a site. When presenting ideas to a client, designer should attend storyboards with a narrative about the task that the customer intends to accomplish. The spaces of information architecture, navigation design, graphic design and usability performance assessment overlap. Conventional human computer interface design is refers to as primarily navigation design and usability evaluation, with a touch of information architecture and graphic design.

A site map is a sophisticated diagram that shows the overall elements of a Web site. Some Web site map may exhibit the structure of a Web site that helps people to find online cheap transaction and electronic coupons. The storyboards depict the steps a customer would negotiate to achieve a task. In addition, some storyboard may exhibit how a customer interacts with a Web site that permits group of colleagues to locate, recommend, and share idea or things with each other. The spaces of information architecture, navigation design, graphic design and usability performance assessment overlap. Conventional human computer interface design epitomizes primarily navigation design and usability evaluation, with a touch of information architecture and graphic design. A site map is a sophisticated diagram that shows the overall organization of a Web site. Some Web site map may exhibit the structure of a Web site that helps people to find online cheap transaction and electronic coupons.

The storyboards depict the steps a customer would negotiate to achieve a task. In addition, some storyboard may exhibit how a customer interacts with a Web site that permits group of colleagues to locate, recommend, and share idea or things with each other. The fonts, colors, and layout are preparatory, not signifying a final decision, but instead giving the graphic designer suggestion about which information needs to encounter highlight or grouped together. One probably noticed that the illustrations of site maps, storyboards, and schematics here appear pretty basic. At this phase they are just abstract representations, not to be taken literally. Their position is to get the big idea across, without the irrelevant details that distract reviewers. The design teams clean up sketched representations by building electronic version before showing these representations to clients or customers. Others are happy showing the informal, sketched representations to get earlier validation and keep the discussion focused on the important issues. This really depends on the clients and their expectations. If an organization manages their expectations well, clients will understand why the organization is showing them rough sketches.

The site designers often create prototypes quickly and they timely employ it to obtain feedback from customers. Low-fidelity prototyping is one technique that many design teams use to achieve this task. In low fidelity prototyping, design teams utilize paper, whiteboards, Post-it notes, and markers to construct rough cuts of a Web site. Sketches are low fidelity when they are far from the final design in both their visual and interactive details. In addition to sketching, design teams can use cut, copy, and paste techniques with scissors, glue, and photocopying machines. Several design teams use a set of low-fidelity pages; they can test a design with representative customers and obtain their feedbacks. Several organizations sit representative customers down in front of the sketches and ask how they would complete a particular task. Based on the customer's verbal responses or pointing, one of the teammates can play computer and flip to a new page to show the designed output of the site. Observing what customers do on these low fidelity designs will give design teams valuable information about how to refine early design ideas. This type of prototyping and testing can let design teams iterate through an entire cycle of design, prototype, and evaluate in less than a day.

At least 10 to 20 times easier and faster to create a low-fidelity prototype than an equivalent high-fidelity (hi-fi) prototype. By high-fidelity prototype, they mean one that looks polished and complete, shaped with computer-based tools such as Macromedia Dreamweaver or Adobe Photoshop. Pragmatic experience has shown that it is at least 10 to 20 times easier and quicker to construct a low-fidelity prototype than an equivalent high-fidelity prototype. The high-fidelity prototype refers to one that looks elegant and comprehensive, produced with computer-based tools such as Macromedia Dreamweaver or Adobe Photoshop. I am not advocating that you do not need hi-fi prototypes-just that you do not need them in the early stages of design. It is not worth the effort of concentrating on colors, fonts, and alignment when there are more imperative problems like organization and overall site structure to contemplate. Another value of low fidelity prototypes is that because exact programming or graphic design proficiency are not required, they integrate the insights and contributions of each team member into the design. Several scholars have seen even chief executive officers creating low fidelity prototypes. Creating low fidelity prototypes and evaluating them with customers elicits teambuilding experience, customer relationship, even for people with roles that customarily do not encompass interaction with customers. By doing this, online entity will involve everyone on the same page about what customers really need. Online organization will discover that this process is more effective, profitable and fun to create the low fidelity prototypes than to argue continuously about what customers might want.

Chapter 23

Managers of the online organizations should evade Computer-Based Tools in the initial design stages. Research demonstrates that designers who work out conceptual thoughts on paper have a propensity to iterate more and explore the design space more broadly, while designers using computer-based tools tend to take only one idea and work it out in detail. The findings from various studies states that the conversation is qualitatively different when designer evaluate people with a high-fidelity prototype. For example, clients frequently respond with articulations like, I do not prefer your color structure or these two buttons need to be arranged accurately.

When presented with a low-fidelity prototype, however, clients are prone to articulate something such as, these labels on the navigation bar do not make sense to me, or I have been missing a link to the shopping cart here on this page. In other words, with low-fidelity prototypes, which may be deficient in irrelevant details like color, font, and alignment to distract the eye, people concentrates on the communication and on the overall site structure.

All of the tools used in Web design today concentrate on constructing finished products. Tools like Microsoft FrontPage, Adobe GoLive, and Macromedia Dreamweaver assist organization to create production Web sites, not early prototypes. What an excellent idea to generate a paper prototyping kit, this is use for creating paper prototypes that everyone on design teams can access. The followings are list of the supplies paper prototyping kit: (a) loads of paper, both white and colored construction paper, (b) lots of index cards, (c) lots of post-its, and (d) transparencies. In addition, (a) scotch tape (b) Scissors, (c) an exact knife, (d) paste, try not to eat too much of it, (e) Markers with lots of colors, (f) pens, (g) rulers, and (h) duct tape.

The following lists are the technological tool use by designers for creating Web design: (1) Microsoft Visio, (2) Macromedia, (3) Director, (4) Adobe Illustrator, and (5) Adobe Photoshop. This aforementioned tool lists concentrates on finished products and they contain some kind of identical glitch. Until tools that generate and support the progression from low-fidelity to high fidelity prototypes become widely available, I am advocating that practitioner delay using computer-based tools. Incidentally, there is a developed quality tool called DENIM that allows company to draft low-fidelity prototypes on a computer. When the organizations are ready, they should switch to Computer-Based Tools. When should the online organization shift to computer-based tools? This is contingent on the organization work practices. The organization must absolutely save designs and e-mail them to others thus they are ready. Meanwhile, design teams frequently want to switch to using a computer when they are making presentation to clients. The general principle would encourage organization not show low-fidelity sketches to clients because they would perceive it as unprofessional. However, high-fidelity mock-ups are time consuming to create, and again they have the side effect of directing the discussion toward extremely fine details. One resolution is to administer with sketches and, as earlier mentioned, manage client' expectations by demonstrating that your organization utilizes sketches instead of computer-based designs to speed up the iteration process and to focus on the important issues at this stage.

Another solution for high-fidelity shortcoming is to use what practitioner term as medium-fidelity prototypes. Medium-fidelity prototypes possess several more details about content, but they do not divert clients or customers with fonts, colors, and graphics. Medium-fidelity prototypes are excellent concession if an organization need to present mock-ups. At some material time the design team will have most of the major structural and interaction issues solved and satisfactorily tested with customers. This is a right time to create high-fidelity prototypes-ones that are richer and closer to what the final site will resemble and feel like. Design teams will probably create them with HTML and graphic design tools such as Illustrator and Photoshop. Again, the solution here is to fake it. For instance, suppose the site permits people view stock prices. They do not have to show the real prices, or even real graphs. Just generate one or two sample images and use them for all of the graphs. Organization will show enough content to give people the feel of the final site. As another example, if design teams are building a site that uses personalization technology to improve the customer experience, when applying PERSON-ALIZED CONTENT (D4) organization might mock up the customization at this stage and makes it look the same for all of their test participants.

In the initial stages of design, organization often want to generate prototypes that show a broad swath of what the final Web site will support. These horizontal prototypes might depict the top-level pages, but with out much depth behind them. The homepage might have all the links that an entity deserve to have, and each will take the user somewhere, but any links from those second-level pages that implement precise features will not exist yet. These prototypes are excellent for ensuring that the basic features of the site are present and organized logically. In contrast, sometimes an online organization will want to flesh out and test the steps that a customer will navigate through to complete a particular task, such as SIGNIN/NEW ACCOUNT (H2).

A vertical prototype implements only the key pages along the path for finishing a precise task. This step is right because the understanding of the complex feature is poor or the feature needs further exploration. Online organization will not yet support any links that connect to other tasks or other parts of the site. Online organizations often want to merge these two techniques. Prototype embraces the entire top level of the site with a horizontal prototype to depict a flavor of what will appear on the site. Then the practitioner should focus on one specific feature, and use the vertical approach to prototype the pages illustrating that feature in detail.

There are some negative aspects to using prototypes. Many people have confidence that creating prototypes takes time away from structuring the actual site. The value of generating and assessing *rapid* prototypes must become what the organization articulate to the vast customers. In addition, although prototypes are helpful for obtaining some types of information, however, they are not as effective for estimating download speeds and excellence of customer service. Finally, when using medium- and high-fidelity prototypes, design teams have to manage customers or client expectations. Seeing something that looks and feels like it is working can make customers and clients think about the finality of the Web site design. Any members of the organization will have to explain that the prototypes still represent initial stages of design; hence, things are still open to change. Web site evaluation is the third segment of iterative design. Organization should not overlook and ensure compliant with Web site evaluation. This evaluation permits organization to determine if they are meeting the target goals. Several organizations evaluate their Web sites through the assistance of third party experts reviews. These are the Web site evaluation responsibilities: (a) permitting experts to assess, (b) informal testing with few participant, (c) heuristic evaluation, and (d) formal study of customers. An expert review does not involve customers and this is an effective strategy for evaluating Web sites. The most common expert review is refers to as heuristic evaluation.

The Web guru Jacob Nielsen is the man that developed heuristic evaluation. The pragmatic idea is have three to five expert judges independently appraise a Web site, the evaluator should utilize a list of usability heuristics or principles. Nielsen's site, www.useit.com lists ten such heuristics. In a heuristic evaluation, the evaluators go through the site, often with a set of sample tasks as a guide, their responsibility is to search for violations of the heuristics. They are supposed to note each violation and make a suggestion for fixing it. For example, if an evaluator found that a site used different terminology for the same concept on different pages in the site, the evaluator would document a "consistency" violation and suggest using one of the terms on each page. The evaluators are responsible to rate each violation with a level of severity. Severity levels are usually assessed on the basis of how violation will impact prospective customers and frequency of the violation.

To facilitate Web site prototype, design teams should ask customers to do some of the tasks from the task analysis, while design teams take good notes. The entire goal is to acquire qualitative feedback from customers about what works and what does not, both from what they articulate and from what they actually do. To maximize the varieties of the prototype, the prototype does not have to be computer based. The common piece of paper is an adequate prototype. In this case, compel customers to point and click with their fingers, just as they would do with a mouse. According to several scholars, one might recruit several representative customers to come to the offices and the management will ask them to complete the tasks with the prototype. Alternatively, design teams might visit customers in their homes or offices and ask them to do the same. Previous to the period an organization commences, they should ask participants to apply their thought process aloud, to declare what is going on in their minds. This is term as think-aloud, verbal, and protocol.

The customers will perhaps find doing this a little eccentric at first, but they will acclimatize to it quickly. The organization may have to inspire them every so often by asking a question like, so what are you looking for now? The data accumulated in informal evaluations is qualitative process data. This kind of data provides an overall gestalt feeling for what works and what is not functional. While participants encounter this assessment, organization should glance for occurrences in which they appear confused, say something negative, or even swear. These are term critical incidents. Organizations may employ the critical incidents as a starting point for places they will redesign.

Chapter 24

In an online environment, managers are often observant for positive incidents, cases in which the customer liked the site or things appeared to be going smoothly. Positive incidents elicits a hint about which parts of organizational design work well, and so that organization might be able to take advantage of some of the same ideas elsewhere. I am not recommending that you use informal evaluation techniques to indicate that one Web site design is better than another, or to say how long certain actions will take. Instead, use the results to categorize potential glitch areas that need to be improved. After you think you have resolved the glitches, repeat the tests with a new set of representative customers and see if the glitches have been addressed properly.

The goals of formal usability studies might be the expectation of customer ability to register and create an account in less than two minutes. Organization may decide to run this study with as few as ten participants, though it usually takes more participants when organization wants to test numerical goals. The category of information to collect in this condition is quantitative bottom-line data. Bottom-line data comprises of hard numerical metrics where organization are searching for statistical significance-a serious and dependable difference instead of one due to chance. Bottom-line data is particularly significant for easy, recurring communications, such as, are customers finishing the task quicker when this button is located on the left or right side of the page. This type of data is also helpful for comparing two dissimilar interfaces, such as, can vast people successfully makes acquisitions and check out utilizing shopping cart interface A or B. Online testing makes it simple to test a diversity of similar issues. This testing lets organization to recruit and test various participants online to attain statistical accuracy quickly. Several companies proffer products to set up and run online tests. These sites know how to recruit research participants for any organization, or allow business enterprise to enter a list of e-mail addresses from current customers or client organization own participant pool. The sites then automatically e-mail research participants, guide them to a test site, and ask them to answer tasks questionnaires that client organization has defined in advance. Most site systems allow organization to track and document the pages the participants go through, as well as ask survey questions. Some practitioners have developed innovative and potentially controversial-ways to measure the metrics of usability. One Web site study used "revisit to the homepage" as an indication of an error. The implication was that consumers got lost on the Web site and had to go back to the homepage. This might be a big assumption without additional data to back it up. What if customers desire to revisit to the homepage because they have completed navigation on particular section? If you want to measure the number of errors, ascertain that you define errors earlier and that everyone agrees on the definition. All organization should incorporate multiple techniques and also the expertise of the professional that conduct expert reviews, informal evaluations, and formal evaluations. The techniques to adopt should be synonymous with organization cost constraints, as well as by how early in the process the evaluation is taking place. For instance, testing low fidelity prototypes is especially effective in very early stages. In later stages, because there is availability of site details, design teams might want to create HTML prototypes instead so that organization can evaluate these details.

Organization should constantly run expert reviews and informal evaluations as they iterate, to work out basic design problems. Focus especially on qualitative process data in the early stages of design because this helps design teams figure out the location of the big problems. Organization should use the patterns to administer solutions to these problems and then iterate. A sound idea is to do a few formal assessments as the Web site matures, as it gets closer to deployment, or even after it has been in operation. This approach will help Organization to refine and polish the Web site. Sometimes utilizing five to ten test participants will be excellent enough to convince the organization and members of the teammates that the problems found during testing are legitimate design issues that must be resolved. However, it will frequently be harder to persuade management or the marketing organization that the design teams need to make changes, particularly on a high-traffic page like the homepage. In that case, employ more formal usability studies and techniques, such as online usability testing, which makes it simple to test the site quickly with 50 to 200 customers. The solution to designing flourishing Web sites is a customer-centered, iterative procedure that first discovers the prospective customers and their responsibilities. Every organization should follow the principles of involving the customers, while designers conduct rapid prototyping, and assessment design to create design ideas and prototypes that the organization evaluate with real customers. The assessment always leads to redesign and the organization should replicate the iterative process until they accomplish usability and business goals. An organization should permit customers to participate throughout design development phase in order to have appropriate design. The responsibilities of the management are to set the team's usability goals early in the design process and frequently assess the progress toward these organizational goals. The iterative design process will enhance the Web site design at the minimum cost. The monitoring process should ensue when the Web site is finalize, the organization should continuously monitor the customer metrics in order to decipher the accomplishments, to inform changes and to set future goals for the next version of the Web site.

The readers of this book should encourage their organization to incorporate customer centered design, iterative process, customer involvement, and encourage design teams to conduct prototyping evaluation with real customers. In order to maximize the profitability Web site, knowledgeable individual should embark on a campaign that will advance creating usability goals early in design process and also evaluate progress attainment towards these goals. The organization designing a Web site should reach agreement with customer on iterative design and customer preferences. The online managers should have monthly monitoring of customer metric, conduct site review by someone other than the designers and obtain site performance metrics. The correction of any glitch will involve participation of representative customers in order ensure the accuracy of design iterative and set goals for new site. This is a clarion call to convince the members of the organization that iterative design permits low cost and enhance Web site, which will eventually encourage customer revisit.

The patterns, principles, and techniques of customer-centered design are hereby included in the framework of a complete Web site design process. The organization should follow a sketch to designing, implementing, and maintaining a Web site. Any Web site design should contain the advantages of being useful, usable, reliable and satisfying site customers. The organization goal is contain in the general process and provision for creating and updating a Web site, something that enable one to focus the precious time and energy on clear goals. Organization should have availability of a well-defined process because this is useful for the organizational clients. A well-defined process informs consumers about what they can expect from the organization and what organization need from customers to build a Web site that meets their expectations and the needs of the customers. The design process will not always go as easily as described here. It is iterative; that is, it repeats and it jumps back and forth when essential. Nor will this process resolve all your glitches. Acclimatize it to your team, your project, and your organization. Formal procedures that are essential for large teams may be overkill for small teams. Techniques that function for art centered design firms are unlikely to work for e-commerce-centered design firms. The following definitions have been advanced; the term customer epitomize any individual who will utilize the Web site the organization is designing, such as, business site, government site, customer site, employee site, administrator site and partner site. The term clients exemplify people dispensing the funding and the people whom the organization is performing the work.

The development of a Web site can be broken down into seven segments, such as, discovery: this represents the target customer needs, the business goals and customer goals for the Web site. Exploration: this is a process of generating several rough primary Web site designs, out of which one or more will win priority for further development. Refinement: this is a process of polishing the navigation, layout, and flow of the selected design. Production represents the practice of developing a fully iterative prototype and creates a design specification. Implementation: this denotes the routine of developing the code, content, and images for the Web site. Launch: this is a process of deploying the Web site for actual use. What is the importance of maintenance processes and why focus on customer-centered Web design? This is a powerful means for supporting the existing site, gathering and examining metrics of success, and preparing for the next redesign. The primary four steps that organization should adopt are the following: (a) discovery via production, (b) focus on the overall design of a Web site, and (c) characterize the customer activity on the Web site and how they accomplish it.

The online organization sometimes typify the above four steps as the design process. They sometimes engage each by rapid iteration, with progressive modification and moving the design from high-level and general to increasingly specific and detailed. During these stages online organization has found that the additional time designers spend up front in the rigid reiterations, the more likely it is that the Web site will meet customer assurances. In the discovery phase a team might repeat five to ten times or more on paper. As the team advances into the electronic representations used in the refinement stage, it might iterate or reiterate much less, perhaps only three or four times. The exact number of iterations are contingents on how well the design performs when evaluated. Punctuate each of the first four steps with a demonstration to the client. Hand over all agreed-upon deliverables at this time, such as a site map, a high-level diagram of a Web site, or a specification document detailing what the Web site will do when it is completed.

Chapter 25

The major point of the presentation, though, is to attain approval about the work the organization performed during that phase. The organization, as a developer of customer-centered site, should only exhibit presentation of what has now become an ongoing dialogue with the client. The concept indicated that there are many stakeholders in the design process, such as, the client and the target customers. At many points in the process, the recommendation to the design teams should include reporting back to the client to confirm if the design process is in compliance.

Organization has an excellent opportunity to assess their existing Web site, as well as to evaluate and crosscheck competitor' Web sites for opportunities to enhance and distinguish their own site from competitors. One of the most essential patterns that come into play here is the UP-FRONT VALUE PROPOSITION (C2). The value proposition states what the Web site proffers to the target customers. Some methods that will productive at this stage include interview, thus, an organization goal is to explain iterative design and providing commentary pertinent to value proposition persuasively to someone on the street, in one sentence. Everything online organizations embed on the Web site should draws on the single idea of the theme that unifies the site. If an organization is creating a new Web site, the management needs the thought process to decipher the value proposition carefully, making several site drafts before deciding on the best one. Conversely, if an organization is updating or redesigning an existing Web site, the management may need to reconsider the existing value proposition. In either case the UP-FRONT VALUE PROPOSITION (C2) pattern provides steps for creating the right one. Online organizations are bound to consider branding notion at the early design phase. They also want customers to think of the brand when they contemplate about the organizational Web site. The impression an online organization wants customers to have after visiting their site includes, reliability, trustworthy, exciting and fun. The SITE BRANDING (EI) pattern provides exercises to assist an online organization decide what kind of impressions to leave with customers.

The PERSONALIZED CONTENT (D4) patterns elicit some starting points. For example, if online entity is working on an e-commerce site, they should consider how personalization could help the vast customers find interesting and useful products. Maybe the entity Web site can recommend products, or maybe it can let people see a list of the most popular items. If the organization design teams are developing a news site, perhaps the visitors can specify zip codes to get local news and weather. Internationalized and localized content pattern speaks about the zip codes, this is a respectable time to convey the issue of internationalization because some countries outside of the United States do not use zip codes. Again, it revert to the question of defining your customers. Do you anticipate people from other countries to use your Web site? If so, there are a host of issues to contemplate, including currency, color, icons, and layout. In order to avoid failure; organization should not permit the propensity to skip the discovery phase. Some clients may insist on skipping the discovery stage and jump straight to Web site development. The responsibility of online design entity is to first determine that the discovery phase is exclusively contained in the scope of the project, the contract and the needs of the customers. The online organization should avoid the concept of Gold-Plating the Web Site. The term Gold-Plating epitomizes the propensity to get the Web site attains absolute perfection before deploying it. Everyone have probably visited vast Web sites, observed some excellent graphic, and they kept rehearsing it in their minds, the organization should incorporate this on the Web site too. Usually that excellent graphic is technically complex and fun to design and implement but, frankly, may not be very helpful to customers. Organization can avoid this dilemma by receiving continuous feedback from customers about what is useful and what is not, and prioritizing the features based on that feedback. This strategy will help organization cut through the mess of features and keep design teams focused on what needs to incorporate on site. The organizations are not supposed to develop and deploy all the features simultaneously. They should deploy the features in phases, in several small steps instead of one big leap. They should plan for future growth, but also plan for the next deployment. The organizations should get the Web Site basics right first. The last thing to watch out for is not taking care of the fundamentals first. This becomes an issue when they design things out of order.

An organization has an issue when they design things out of order. For example, for e-commerce sites it is not logical to design and implement PERSONALIZED RECOMMENDA-TIONS (G3) or a RECOMMENDATION COMMUNITY (G4) if there are still dilemma with the SHOPPING CART (F3) and the QUICK-FLOW CHECKOUT (FI). Resolves the things that the Web site absolutely must have before adding the feature that makes it look sophisticated. The design teams may create the following main documents as an outcome of discovery phase: (a) the customer analysis document, (b) the business analysis document, and (c) the specification document. The Customer Analysis Document grants the design team and the client a deep understanding of and compassion for the Web site's proposed customers. Organization sometimes gives intended customers a foretaste of the Web site offering by describing their characteristics, their needs, and their tasks. The following strategies are profitable, for instance, (a) motivating of customers to visit the Web site, (b) apply UP-FRONT Value PROPOSITION (C2) (c) a task analysis of the intended customers, (d) describing the people task, (e) recognize the technologies they use, and (f) understand social and organizational issues.

One increasingly prevalent way to accomplish this is by creating personas, or highly detailed fictional people, who are descriptive of the consumers. Giving the customers' names makes it easier to communicate about the consumers. Business Analysis Document – This document signify the business needs of the client and the business goals of the Web site. The business analysis document investigates how the goals of the client map to the tasks. The business analysis document records the information that customers revealed during the task analysis. For example, assuming the client's goal for an intranet site is to be the primary source to locate the information of the company. This goal is not meaningful to an administrative assistant whose task is just searching for the information he/she needs to get the job done. If an online organization is revising an existing Web site, a new business examination is probably not necessary, but it is still a good idea to check every so frequently that the business goals are the right goals, and that the Web site works toward those goals. A business analysis document frequently includes the Business plan: The business plan explains the business goals of the Web site and the client's needs. The desired goal contain in the business plan are characterize as the following, (a) how to support existing customers, (b) convert new customers by displaying information about products, and (c) maximizing sales by facilitating purchase online.

The competitive analysis find out the features that competitors have on their Web sites and it recognizes which features are significant to customers and which are not. The competitive analysis also discusses the competitive advantages that the planned Web site will have over others, and the organization then expresses these advantages as high-level goals.

The metrics for success supply the answers to the questions of how to measure the success for both the business and the competitive goals of the online organization. For example, online organization must know the population of customers that the site needs to accumulate in order stay in business. Just as significant as attracting customers is retaining them. Organization must keep customers coming back for more products. Organization must be aware of how many are the repeat customers. They must know what the conversion rate is, or how many visitors become paying customers. They must be aware of how many become community members. Specification document is widely known as a requirements document, the specification document illustrates what the Web site should provide when the work is complete. Specification document explains any functionality the Web site needs, as well as any limitations on the system. At this point, design teams do not have to start thinking about how they will achieve the needed functionality. They should focus instead on what they will accomplish. A specification document contains the following items, such as, (a) project description, (b) common purpose, (c) ultimate goals of the project, and (d) client and customer perspectives, In addition, this comprises: (a) list of tasks, (b) scenarios, (c) storyboards, and (d) fleshing out the features. Meanwhile, these tasks will form the foundation of the Web site assessments. The quantity of task is contingents on the intricacy of the proposed work. A simple project is efficient with ten to twenty complete tasks, but larger projects will need sufficient items to cover all the proposed features. The design teams should endeavor to label tasks as easy, moderate, or difficult. The Web sites should facilitate the way customers complete all the easy tasks, most of the moderate ones, and some of the difficult ones. The design teams should employ competitive comparisons, as well as surveys and other market research techniques, to acquire this type of information. The design teams organize features into sub-features. For example, a Web site that assist to manage personal information will likely have a contact manager, which allow people to add new contacts, edit existing ones, and search for contacts by name. Each feature also contains a short statement on how to review performance indicator in the final Web site. Overall design goals of the organization implement such things as minimizing the number of errors that customers make on the existing site, decreasing purchasing time, reducing check out time from the shopping cart and execute the site for faster use.

Chapter 26

Metrics is another way to measure whether the team has reached these goals and requirements, for instance, when the design teams execute download time to diminish below 20 seconds for 90 percent of the target customers. The metric states how these features is review in general in the final Web site. The lack of specification is risky; yet, several online designers always pass over this step. A specification document should be concise, formal, and this is useful because it forces one to think through important details and make sure that they make sense and are realistic. A specification document simplifies communication with clients, team members, and encourages a shared vision for what the Web site will be like when completed. Although, specification documents are frequently monotonous to peruse. However, this specification documents should be brief and concise, and use vast diagrams to typify the meaning. They might even make specification documents interesting enough to entice everyone to take the time to peruse it.

During the exploration phase organization will produce and survey several designs. These primary designs frequently do not reveal ideas about color, imagery, and typography. However, they do reveal ideas about site structure and navigation. By the end of exploration, design teams will have several prototypes to present to the client, who prefer and choose one for further development and the client will thereby sign off on the work done. Sometimes a client will want to fund continued development of two sites for further modification before making a final selection. In either case, the selected design should contain evaluation-oriented results that exemplify the propensity at meeting the objective and goals of business, client, and customer.

Normally, an organization will generate medium-fidelity site maps, storyboards, and schematics. The design teams would assess all their designs promptly with target customers to ensure usefulness and usability. The HOMEPAGE PORTAL (CI) pattern explains some of the ways to structure the homepage, as well as what an organization want on their homepage, such as a PRIVACY POLICY (E4) and a STRAIGHTFORWARD SEARCH FORM (J2). The design teams is responsible for: (a) commencing the initial labor on the information architecture, (b) the overall organization of the Web site's content, and organizing site content at exploration phase as well. The BROWSE-ABLE CONTENT (B2) pattern signifies details on how to design and implement the architecture. An organization will present several sets of medium-fidelity site maps, storyboards, and schematics to their client. Each set corresponds to a design option that addresses the issues illustrated by the customer analysis document, the business analysis document, and the specification document. In particular, the storyboards will reveal the primary ideas for how to implement the scenarios in the specification document. However, at this stage none of the deliverables will have much detail; rather they will have just enough detail to represent the general idea. After the organizations have chosen a design idea from the variations presented in the Exploration phase, the design teams will develop the selected idea further. The design teams will have to polish the navigation, layout, and flow of the selected design, supplying a clearer understanding of how the Web site will look and feel. By the end of refinement, organization will have a vastly detailed prototype to present to the client, who they expect will sign off on the work. During the Refinement phase, several organization employs iteratively refine, detail, and informally test the design. They also determine aspects such as the exact typeface of labels and body text, the exact sizes and appearances of images, color schemes and palettes. For most sites the design teams will not find it essential to design every page at this stage because they will break down the site into classes of pages into such things as homepage, second-level pages, and pages for specific types of content. An example, or template, can represent every one of these classes of pages. In this phase, site maps are still intangible illustrations of the entire Web site. Conversely, storyboards and schematics are no longer boring; instead they are now rich with images, contents, icons, typography, and sophisticated color schemes. The major distinction between Refinement and Exploration is that the pattern that design teams create in the Refinement phase has more detail than the pattern they generated during the Exploration phase. Thus, design teams can implement several of the same patterns in both phases. Some patterns are more helpful during Refinement than during Exploration.

For instance, the pattern CLEAR FIRST READS (13) adopts a concept from graphic design, this one proposed to grant a quick first impression of a visual design. This suggests that organization should explicitly design the first thing that a potential customer sees on a Web page to give an overall sense for the content of the page. A related pattern is GRID LAYOUT (II), which gives organization ways of constructing Web pages in a constant and understandable manner. Another pattern to reflect on is MULTIPLE WAYS TO NAVIGATE (BI). People navigate Web sites in several ways, sometimes using a diversity of search mechanisms, text links, buttons, and navigation bars. This pattern illustrate how to provide multiple and sometimes redundant process of navigating, to make it easier to locate the right page. An organization has the capabilities to deliver one set of medium- to high-fidelity deliverables, such as, site maps, storyboards, and schematics to the client. These deliverables are analogous to the ones in the Exploration phase, but they contain greater detail. For example, the site maps depict the overall site structure in detail, and the storyboards and schematics employ more of graphical images and color. In the production phase, the goal is to construct a detailed set of deliverables that represent the final design idea. The deliverables, including interactive prototypes, written narratives, guidelines, and specifications, are high-fidelity and contain as much detail as possible about the layout, navigation, visuals, and content for each Web page. Precisely what they deliver at the conclusion of this phase depends on whether one will continue to the next phase (Implementation) or hand off the design to someone else. If an organization will hand off the design, then make the interactive prototypes and specifications precise and exceedingly detailed so that there is no uncertainty about what the next team will implement. One may want to call for more assessment during implementation to guarantee that the specification is free of errors. The client should examine the ongoing improvement to catch any problems before the new team exacts too much work. Ideally, though, the design teams are known to work in unison with the engineering, art, marketing, editorial, and management teams so that the site is implemented as designed and tested, and so that the unavoidable questions that arise can be answered.

During the Production phase, organization should continue to assess the product with real customers. The reason being the first time the new system comes together, often with more complexity than existed in earlier prototypes, new interaction issues may arise. During production the dimension of patterns translate into more low-level as the problems become increasingly technical. For instance, one pattern that they normally incorporate here is ACTION BUTIONS (K4), which demonstrates how to make buttons that appear common household button that people press. Another helpful pattern at this stage is OBVIOUS LINKS (1<10), which discusses why links must be simple to see and elucidates nature of their construction. The deliverables of the Production phase fluctuate from organization to organization. They list the most common ways of relating the design in detail. In contrast to the specification document, the design document explains how the Web site functions in great detail. The public is now aware that all of the features from the specification document are included and uses site maps, storyboards, and schematics to explain the flow of interaction. If design teams work terminates here and they hand the project off to another team, the design document needs to be detailed, descriptive, and unambiguous. If the same design teams continue to do implementation, the design document may not need to be so comprehensive. Let the organization provide sufficient information that the client and the team will understand. Frequently delivered along with the design document, an interactive prototype gives the organization and their client a solid foundation for how the finished Web site will appear and behave. Several designers are fond of creating interactive prototypes by employing standard Web site production tools, such as Adobe GoLive or Macromedia Dreamweaver, as well as with proto typing tools such as Macromedia Director. The suggestion is to provide enough detail that everyone can see and how the final Web site will look and feel. For example, not all of the links have to operate correctly, provided it is clear in what they do. Some firms deliver interactive prototypes instead of a design document but embed several details as annotation to the prototype. For instance, moving the mouse across certain sections of the prototype might download a specification of the font family and size.

The design teams are responsible to insert technical stipulations in the document, which includes things like the kind of Web server, the kind of programming and scripting languages, the kind of database, and what kind of the version of HTML to employ. They sometime comprise performance metrics with the total number of people the organization is simultaneously supporting. Optionally, the technical specifications might include some engineering prototypes as a proof of the concept this represent that the complex parts of the proposed design are technically possible and design teams can create it. These guidelines are the broad rules for designers to follow on every Web page and this diminishes inconsistencies between pages.

Chapter 27

The online organization shall make necessary effort to have a clear design guideline and make it obvious on key web pages. A design guideline should describe the following: (a) the excellent fonts that design teams can use, (b) the color the links should be, (c) when the symbol should be used and where it should be located, (d) what color format to use, and (e) what the highest file size of each Web page is, and so on. The person who will execute and/or sustain the Web site should be able to understand and use the guidelines. Optionally, the guidelines might also comprise a style guide to guarantee that the writing is consistent throughout the Web site, for instance, using the term email instead of e-mail. Web page templates are the HTML files that symbolize typical Web pages on the site. The objective of using these templates is to avoid contradictions between pages. With a smallest amount of effort, organization can copy and amend these templates with content specific for a particular page. The following are the six patterns that are valuable to consider when one is developing Web page templates: (1) PAGE TEMPLATES (D1), (2) GRID LAYOUT (II), (3) ABOVE THE FOLD (12), (4) CLEAR FIRST READS (13), (5) EXPANDING-WIDTH SCREEN SIZE (14), and (6) SITE ACCESSBILITY (B9). In the implementation phase, the organization should focus on the goals to create the HTML, images, database tables, and software necessary for a polished and fully functional Web site that will be in operation and used by its target customers. In order to accomplish this goal, the concept encourages running formal usability tests to ensure that customers can complete the tasks they want to achieve. The quality assurance groups are responsible to test all the code, graphics, and HTML thoroughly so that the Web site would functions as intended and downloads quickly. The design teams must check all the content for correctness at this stage. Let organization devote more effort to content in the implementation phase.

Two patterns that come in handy here are WRITING FOR SEARCH ENGINES (D6) and DISTINCTIVE HTML TITLES (D9) they are available to help scrutinize the internal structure of Web pages for search engines and for customers. Another constructive pattern is INVERSE PYRAMID WRITING STYLE (D7), which implement technology for making text content easier to skim and faster to read. The valuable pattern for constructing a content management system is CONTENT MODULES (D2), which puts content in a database to keep production costs down and site reliability high.

The tools useful at this stage include an amendment control system for storing and sharing files between a group of people, and a bug database for tracking glitches. Choose tools that you already understand how to manipulate and that have been proven to work. The Implementation phase of development is an awkward time to test an unknown product. However, do scrutinize new tools between projects, in order to keep your skills sharp and up-to-date. Organization needs to determine naming conventions for folders and files. For instance, the folder that designs teams will employ to contain the site images. They may consider using one folder or many. If there are organizational products for sale, the proper name of each product will be CLEAN PRODUCT DETAILS (F2) page. Several organizations set the naming conventions up to make it easy for updating new product pages in the future. If organization is using SECURE CONNECTIONS (E6), they may need to apply for digital certificates at a certain time.

Digital certificates are a way for Web servers to demonstrate that they authentic. The digital certificates are release by a variety of trusted third-party vendors recognized as certification authorities. Organization may decide to get multiple certificates, for all the Web servers that they will be using. The Web site needs authentic review in this phase to guarantee that it is high quality and professional. This review consists of performing more usability tests, doing some editorial spot-checking, and running automated test suites. The following checklist indicates some of the tests that need to be conducted during implementation phase: (a) check that the Web site contains the entire features, (b) check for stipulation in the specification document, (c) check for correct implementation, and (d) check that the developed Web pages are compatible with various Web browsers. In addition, this includes: (a) confirm for text-only browsers used by the blind, (b) assess that the developed Web pages can be viewed in different monitor sizes, and (c) verify if the Web pages can be downloaded in a reasonable time by people who have slower Internet connections.

The assessment plan spells out what steps will be taken to ensure that the Web site functions as intended. At a minimum, it should comprise checking for performance, spelling, broken links, and the like. It should also explicate how each of the features described in the specification document will be tested. Updates any documents that are obsolete and it should be updated at this time (if they have not been already). This includes the specification document, the design document, design guidelines, and Web page templates. The Launch phase pertains with the live deployment of the Web site. At this point, there is time to implement only insignificant polishing on the Web site, such as checking for misspellings, grammatical errors, broken links, and broken images. All of the significant checks should have been integrated in the previous phase, implementation. Some design teams prefer to roll out the Web site in stages. Instead of embedding the entire Web site at once and waiting until the very end to deploy it, selected parts of the Web site are generated and deployed incrementally. Stress-test the Web site, by simulating hundreds or even thousands of consumers navigating it at the same time, to certify that it still performs reasonably.

The maintenance document articulates in detail how to preserve the completed Web site. This document enlightens about which parts of the Web site maintains periodic update, how often they need this update, and who should update them. Furthermore, the same document should also describe the database tables, showing how they fit together. The launch phase deals with the live operations of the Web site. At this point, there is time to do only minor polishing on the Web site, such as, inspecting for misspelling, grammatical errors, broken links, and broken images. All of the major assessment belongs to the implementation phase. During the inauguration phase organization should construct the most significant functions and sub-sites first, and place them on a beta Web site for early adopters. Meanwhile, they should utilize the ensuing feedback to drive the immediate design and development of the rest of the Web site. Design teams should handle staged development carefully, they should avoid displaying the Web site too early because it may exhibits a lack of polish, and thus, prospective customers may avoid the site later. Several design teams find a postmortem a useful exercise after launch, to assess what things went right, what did not, why; and how to avoid these predicaments in the future. Maintenance is perhaps the most abandoned aspect of Web site design.

The purpose of the maintenance phase is to accomplish all of the activities required to sustain a Web site. Beyond basic tasks such as updating the site with new content and promptly answering customer e-mail maintenance includes the following: (a) changing code, (b) fixing bugs, (c) collecting usability, and (d) satisfaction metrics. In addition, this includes: (a) verifying that all links point to valid pages, (b) checking that there are no spelling errors, (c) or grammatical errors, and (d) ensuring that pages in the Web site follow the design guidelines. Organization should periodically back up the entire Web site into a safe place located in a distant building. Organization should update the

FREQUENTLY ASKED QUESTIONS (H7) PAGES. They should check that the team is WRITING FOR SEARCH ENGINES (D6). They should maintain server logs that show where people come from, what search terms they use (see ORGANIZED SEARCH RESULTS (J3)), and what they are doing on the site Maintenance. The responsibilities of the management includes assessing the Web site, collecting measurements on how customers use the Web site, analyzing and summarizing the metrics they collect, and ensuring metrics availability to the rest of the team and the company. Metrics element is refers to as one of the most important parts of maintaining a Web site. Metrics denotes the heartbeat of a Web site, measuring its overall health. Without metrics, design teams cannot tell which aspects are functional or not. The maintenance phase is the extensive part of the design cycle. Consequently, organization should start involving maintenance phase during the budget development because maintenance phase is most expensive.

To conduct a revision to the web site, an organization may want to perform a minor change or renovate of the web site. Online organization conducting web site revision are advise to employ metrics, wisdom, and knowledge they gain from developing and managing the old web site in order to ascertain that the new web site will succeed. Minor redesigns or additions to the existing site can go through an accelerated development process. One thing is important, design teams do not have to revisit such things as the business analysis document. However, design teams should pay attention to the specification document, the design document, and the design guidelines. They should focus on the goal of keeping the web site consistent throughout. Some design teams insist on making their work look dissimilar from the rest of the web site. Except an extremely compelling reason exists, organization should insist on maintaining a consistent look and feel for the entire web site to make it easier for customers. Alternatively, complete overhauls denote going through the entire web site development process again. Comprehensive redesigns materializes when major changes are needed, such as when customer expectations change, when customer behavior changes, when there are new technology considerations, when fresh content and functionality are indispensable, or when the web site becomes outdated. The organization should obtain customer feedback before embarking on the final switch to a new web site. One of the excellent ways to run usability tests on the new site is to substantiate that customers can complete the essential tasks.

Chapter 28

An additional way is to embed a link on the homepage in order to permit customers to try out the new site while requesting their preferences. If organization has a list of e-mail addresses, they can contact their customers to inform them that the Web site will encounter an update soon. The final option of getting feedback is through virtual testing. In this case a small sample customer will see the updated Web site instead of the regular Web site.

An organization has an advantage to compare the transaction that their customers conduct on the new Web site to what they do on the regular Web site to observe if any interesting new strengths or weaknesses are apparent with the new site. For example, Amazon.com and Google use this technique quite successfully. Organization can use online surveys for this purpose as well.

According to deliverables concept, all periodic Web sites metrics commences from the business analysis document created in the discovery phase. For example, they consist of the following: (a) total number of visitors hits (b) customers conversion rate (c) customers satisfaction metrics, and (d) usability evaluations. Bug reports are the followings: (a) customer e-mails, (b) Web site evaluations, and (c) server log file are excellent process to find bug reports.

Bug reports are what they employ to rate each problem according to severity (such as must fix, should fix, and could fix), and approximate the time to correct the problem. Organization should do periodic backups of the entire Web site as a security against accidental deletion of file, the Web server are sabotaged or the anomalies of hackers on the Web site.

Organization should stockpile the backup in detach warehouse different from the facility that houses the Web server, in case of an inclement disaster like flood or fire. The organization process, structure and strategy should ascertain that their Web site meet the preferences of the clients and the customers. The organization should execute the strategies of customer-centered design and iterative prototyping in every step and prior to the Web site final production. The important lesson here is to make certain that organization have customer-centered process that is documented, is repeatable and can be enhanced by the organization continuously.

The policy and procedure of this organization need a revision in order to contain the stipulations of Web site consistency with the principle and techniques of meeting the needs of customers, customer centered design and iterative prototyping. I will encourage my organization or any organization to permit the Web site to become paragon of customer centered that is documented, reproducible, and favor continuous improvement over time.

The organization should request the contribution of the customers as appropriate for project evaluation, information architecture, navigation design, graphic design, and following design methodologies and standards. The following are the responsibilities of the management teams: site maintenance, evaluate Web site performance, obtain customers feedbacks, and visits customers in their houses or offices for iterative prototyping. The aforementioned will facilitate the provision of quality products and services to the customers by the Web site in cost effective and timely manner.

The element of pattern contains six segments, such as, name, background, problem, forces, solution and other pattern to ponder. Patterns (Group d) are convenient when the designer desires to improve the search feature on the Web site. Similarly, they also use patterns (Group k) to proffer ease of navigation after the customer indicate problem. Pattern (Group A & B) contains genres and the element that create a navigation framework for the whole Web site. Meanwhile, patterns (Group H) contain the element that assist customer to finish the task on site.

From my experience, I discovered that several organizations have developed graphic user interfaces, this is another form of transferable knowledge via the Web site, for instance, (1) eBay utilizes graphical action button for the find it, (2) they use button such as, register and new to eBay, and (3) Amazon.com also utilizes the graphical buttons for the Web site stores. Patterns elicit community familiarity, knowledge and experience into the entire Web site design. Whenever the images is utilized as links this will affect download speed from the Web site, thus, designer must consider this when creating Web site patterns. In my organization, the management implemented a written plan that concentrates on Web design patterns, customer needs and outlining open door policy to the customers.

When the plan came into effect, online customers responded to the invitation, they came into the office and the management collected information on the needs of the customers, what the customers want on the Web site and the type of personal computer they possess. To facilitate their interest, the potential or current customers always receive shirts and mugs. Eventually, the photograph of management and customers is now a frequent agenda. The benefits gained by the organization are following: (a) environment of open communication, (b) high performance culture, (c) accountability, (d) skill for problem solving, and (e) high performance team.

Accordingly, design teams' characteristics are dissimilar

from the customers. Thus, design teams needs to correlate their intuition, behavior and experiences in collaboration with the prospective customers when creating Web sites. In the principle for knowing customers, designer are not the customers, thus they should understand the variable elements, balance the forces, understands customers as people and customers as different. A customer-centered design process advocates that company should have absolute knowledge of the target customers and allows their participation throughout the design process. Organization must learn customer skills, knowledge, their technology and aspirations. Organization must assimilate what customers prefer to accomplish and their task on the Web site. In addition, organization must know the technology, software and equipment the customers prefer to use on Web site. Furthermore, successful organization Web site must assimilate the work, play, life styles, hobby, and social issues of customers. Thus, design teams with solid understanding of these customer' variables and attributes will be in a good position to successfully create a profitable Web site design.

The principle for knowing individual customers entails acknowledging that design teams are not regarded as customers because of dissimilarity between the design team and customer experiences, they differ in thought processes and they are not similar in articulation. The customers and design team discharge activities differently. According to the concepts, the design teams must balance the capabilities or limitations of the elements and incorporate those elements in the final Web design.

The design teams must comprehend and incorporate element, such as, target customer, their skills, their knowledge, customer tasks, technology available to customers, needs, customer social and organizational context (Leedy, & Ormrod, 2005; Douglas, et al., 2002; Lopuck, 2001). An organization that intends to revise the Web site embeds surveys forms on existing Web site purposely to derive feedback from current customers about their preferences. Organization revising their Web site may employ questionnaire to derive information from the target customers that are participating in a focus group. Several organizations constructing new Web site ask the prospective customers for their representation about the competitor' Web sites.

An organization may recruit prospective customers to evaluate and provide right or wrong absolute on the existing Web sites. In order to understand the prospective customers an organization may conduct a focus groups and surveys, by telephone or online, with different types of potential customers, can help design team to focus on the kinds of prospective customers who will be attracted to the Web site. An organization should run a pilot test before showing the site to potential customers. Designers may ask their colleagues to evaluate their focus group, survey, or Web site. The colleagues may even correct the wording or procedure on the Web site.

I am recommending that the Web design be pilot tested with colleagues to decipher anomalies before showing the site to potential customers for evaluation. The designers should create a Web site that elicit a winning experience for the organization audience and enhances the organizational profitability. The organization should embark on research, skill, experience, and careful thought process to build a site that maximizes customer retention and revisit. Organization should embark on the principles and best practices that make sites enjoyable to visit and an asset to the organizations they serve.

The Web survey and feedback engine of the organization where I currently work, contain the following statements addressed to the customers: this organization prefer customers input on what they would like to see on their new site. Please use the twenty-four hour telephone to communicate with the management, provide comments below or the email address is optional. The feedback provides organization with the tools and techniques to improve site design systems that maximizes the quality and corresponding effectiveness. According to many scholars, the customer involvement in pattern design is the current best practices; techniques and knowledge organizations need in areas that have the greatest impact on Web sites e-commerce.

References

Bradlow, E.T., & Schmittlein, D. C., (2000). The little engines that could: Modeling the performance of world wide web search engines. *Marketing Science* 19.1, 43-62

Chong, S., & Pervan, G. (2007). Factors influencing the extent of deployment of electronic commerce for small-and medium-sized enterprises. *Journal of Electronic Commerce in Organizations, 5*(1), 1-29. doi:1157661671

Crowder, David; Crowder, Rhonda (2000). *Building a WebSite for Dummies.* IDG Books Worldwide.

Dawson, A., & Hamilton, V, (2006). Optimizing metadata to make high-value content more accessible to Google users. *Journal of Documentation, 62.3 307-327*

Douglas, K., Duyne, V., Landay, J. A., & Hong, J. I., (2002). The design of sites: Patterns, principles, and processes for crafting a customer-centered Web experience. Addison-Wesley.

Deitel, H.M.; Deitel, P.J.; Steinbuhler, K. (2001). *e-Business and e-Commerce for Managers.* Prentice Hall.

Eysenck, M. (2004). *Research methods design of investigations. Psychology: An international perspective.* New York, NY: Psychology Press.

Fox, S. (2008). Internet riches: *The simple money-making secrets of online millionaires.* New York, NY: American Management Association.

Gates, Bill (1999). *Business at the Speed of Thought.* Warner Books.

Galloway, L. (2007). Can broadband access rescue the rural economy? *Journal of Small Business and Enterprise Development, 14,* 641-653. doi: 1381002571

Galloway, L., & Mochrie, R. (2005). The use of ICT in rural firms: A policy-orientated literature review. Info: *The Journal of Policy, Regulation and Strategy for Telecommunications, Information and Media, 7*(3), 33-46. doi: 850972961

Gardner, R. (2007). *Make a fortune promoting other people's stuff online: How affiliate marketing can make you rich* (1st ed.). New York, NY: McGraw-Hill.

Garrity, E., O'Donnell, J., Kim, Y., & Sanders, G. (2007). An extrinsic and intrinsic motivation-based model for measuring consumer shopping oriented web site success. *Journal of Electronic Commerce in Organizations, 5*(4), 18-38. doi: 1522689851

Gengatharen, D. E., & Standing, C. (2005). A framework to assess the factors affecting success or failure of the implementation of government-supported regional e-marketplaces for SMEs. *European Journal of Information Systems, 14,* 417-433. doi: 987724721

Golafshani, N. (2003). Understanding reliability and validity in qualitative research. *The Qualitative Report, 8*(4), 597-606. Retrieved from http://www.nova.edu/ssss/QR/QR8-4/golafshani.pdf.

Griffiths, G. H., & Howard, A. (2008). Balancing clicks and bricks - strategies for multichannel retailers. *Journal of Global Business Issues, 2*(1), 69-75. doi: 1454513921

Guerrero, M. M., Egea, J. M. O., & González, M.V. R. (2007).

Characterization of online shoppers with navigation problems. *Direct Marketing, 1*(2), 102-113. doi: 1519866571

Gofman, A, Moskowitz H. R & Mets, T. (2009) Integrating science into web design: consumer-driven web site optimization. *The Journal of Consumer Marketing*, 26.4 286-298.

Gluhovsky, I. (2009). Customer behavior model for quality-of-service environments with many service levels. *Journal of Electronic Commerce Research*, 10(1), 29-41. doi: 1667036961

Harris, L., & Rae, A. (2009). The revenge of the gifted amateur... be afraid, be very afraid... *Journal of Small Business and Enterprise Development*, 16(14), 964-709 doi:1927011541

Hettche, M., & Walker, P. (2010). B-Harmony: Building small business and small non-profits partnerships that thrive (*A Framework for Collaborative Competition*). Competition forum, 8(1), 86-93. doi: 2174752241

Hodges, H. E., & Kent, T. W. (2007). Impact of planning and control sophistication in small business. *Journal of Small Business Strategy, 17*(2), 75-87. doi: 1180334021

Hong, I. B. (2007). A survey of Web site success metrics used by Internet-dependent organizations in Korea. *Internet Research, 17*, 272-290. doi: 1281932681

Hu, X., & Wu, Y. (2008). Can web seals work wonders for small e-vendors in the online trading environment? A theoretical approach. *International Journal of E-*

Business Research, 4(3), 20-39. doi: 1475965381

Investopedia. (2009). *Profit.* Retrieved May 30, 2009, from
http://www.investopedia.com/terms/p/profit.asp.

Johnston, D. A., Wade, M., & McClean, R. (2007). Does e-
business matter to SMEs? A comparison of the
financial impacts of internet business solutions on
European and North American SMEs. *Journal of
Small Business Management, 45*(3), 354-361.
doi: 1294062421

Jansen, B. J., & Schuster, S. (2011). Bidding on the buying
funnel for sponsored search and keyword advertising.
*Journal of Electronic Commerce Research*12. 1, 1-18.

Jahng, J. (2000). *Successful design of electronic commerce
environments: The role of sense of presence on user
behavior.* (Order No. 9984837, The University of
Wisconsin - Milwaukee). *ProQuest Dissertations and
Theses, ,* 169-169 p. Retrieved from
http://search.proquest.com/docview/304645077?accou
ntid=139631. (304645077).

Karakaya, F., & Stahl, M. (2009). After market entry barriers
in e-commerce markets. *Journal of Electronic
Commerce Research, 10*(3), 130-143.
doi: 1864032831

Khalifa, M. & Liu, V. (2007). Online consumer retention:
contingent effects of online shopping habit and online
shopping experience. *European Journal of
Information Systems*: Including a Special Section on
Healthcare Information, 16(6), 780-792.
doi: 1399647451.

Kartiwi, M., & MacGregor, R. (2007). Electronic commerce
adoption barriers in small to medium-sized
enterprises (SMEs) in developed and developing

countries: A cross-country comparison. *Journal of Electronic Commerce in Organizations, 5*(3), 35-51. doi: 1522689731

Kent, P. & Finlayson, J. M. (2006). *How to make money online with eBay, Yahoo and Google* (1st ed.). Emeryville, CA: McGraw-Hill.

Khattab, A. A., Aldehayat, J., & Stein, W. (2010). Informing country risk assessment in international business. *International Journal of Business and Management, 5*(7), 54. doi:821543352.

Khalifa, M. & Liu, V. (2007). Online consumer retention: contingent effects of online shopping habit and online shopping experience. *European Journal of Information Systems*: Including a Special Section on Healthcare Information, 16(6), 780-792. doi: 1399647451

Laudon, K. C., & Traver, C. G. (2006). *E-commerce, business, technology and society* (3rd ed.). Upper Saddle River, NJ: Prentice Hall.

Leedy, P. D., & Ormrod, J. E. (2005). *Practical research: Planning and design* (8th ed.). Upper Saddle River, NJ: Pearson.

Lightfoot, W. (2003). Multi-channel mistake: The demise of a successful retailer. International *Journal of Retail & Distribution Management, 31*, 220-229. doi: 345186921

Loukis, E., Sapounas, I., & Aivalis, K. (2008). The effect of generalized competition and strategy on the business value of information and communication technologies. *Journal of Enterprise Information Management*, 21(1), 24-38. doi: 1440904631

Lin, C. P., & Ding, C. G. (2006). Evaluating group differences in gender during the formation of relationship quality and loyalty in ISP service. *Journal of Organizational and End User Computing*, *18*(2), 38-62. doi: 1007709521

Lin, Y., & Wu, H. Y. (2008). Information privacy concerns, government involvement, and corporate policies in the customer relationship management context. *Journal of Global Business and Technology*, *4*(1), 79-91. doi: 1524926891

Loghry, J. D., & Veach, C. B. (2009). Enterprise risk assessments: Holistic approach provides companywide perspective. *Professional Safety, 54*(2), 31. doi:200325280

Lopuck, Lisa (2001). *Web Design for Dummies;* Copyright. IDG Books Worldwide.

MacGregor, R. C. (2006). The role of strategic alliances in the ongoing use of electronic commerce technology in regional small business. *Journal of Electronic Commerce in Organizations, 2*(1), 1-14. Retrieved doi: 730820071

MacGregor, R. C., & Vrazalic L. (2006). E-commerce adoption barriers in small businesses and the differential effects of gender. *Journal of Electronic Commerce in Organizations, 4*(2), 1-24. doi: 1011183921

Matlay, H. (2004). E-entrepreneurship and small e-business development: towards a comparative research agenda. *Journal of Small Business and Enterprise Development, 11*(3), 408-414. doi: 715297481

Malaga, R. (2007, July/September). The value of search engine optimization: An action research project at a new e-commerce site. *Journal of Electronic Commerce in Organizations*5.3 (July-Sep 2007): 68-82.

Namamian, F., & Kamari, F. (2012). Trust in electronic commerce: A new model for building online trust in B2C. *International Journal of Operational Management, Marketing and Services, 2*(2), 72-81. Retrieved from http://search.proquest.com/docview/1412865963?accountid=139631

Rayport, Jeffrey; Jaworkski, Bernard J. (2001). *e-Commerce.* New York, NY: McGraw-Hill Higher Education. ISBN 0-07246521-2.

Shaheen, A. N. (2011). *An electronic service quality reference model for designing e-commerce websites which maximizes customer satisfaction.* http://search.proquest.com/docview/874338150?accountid=139631. (874338150).

Turban, Efraim; Lee, Jae; King, David; Chung, H. Michael (2000). *Electronic Commerce, A Managerial Perspective.* Prentice-Hall.

ABOUT THE AUTHOR

Dr. Ebenezer A. Robinson is an author, professor, mentor, motivational speaker, coach, writer, consultant, researcher, advocate for higher education, and is a California State University Alumnus. He holds an MBA and PhD degree in Business Administration and Electronic Commerce. His call is to educate, motivate, preach, communicate, train and empower others for life success. Dr. Robinson has over 30 years of Corporate America experience in government, industry, business, entrepreneurship, education, consulting, executive director, management accounting, and training. He had published over 5 books and presented 5 papers at several professional and scholarly meetings. As a researcher, he has over ten scientific publications to his credit.

The Principles of Modern Web Design

www.ingramcontent.com/pod-product-compliance
Lightning Source LLC
Chambersburg PA
CBHW071151050326
40689CB00011B/2071